THE DANCE AND THE RAILROAD

AND

FAMILY DEVOTIONS

TWO PLAYS BY
DAVID HENRY HWANG

★

★

DRAMATISTS
PLAY SERVICE
INC.

THE DANCE AND THE RAILROAD
Copyright © 1983, David Henry Hwang

FAMILY DEVOTIONS
Copyright © 1982, 1983, David Henry Hwang

All Rights Reserved

ABOUT THE AUTHOR

David Henry Hwang is the author of *FOB* (1981 Obie Award, Best New Play; Drama-Logue Award), *The Dance and the Railroad* (Drama Desk Nomination, CINE Golden Eagle Award), *Family Devotions* (Drama Desk Nomination), *The House of Sleeping Beauties,* and *The Sound of a Voice* (Drama-Logue Award), all of which were produced at the New York Shakespeare Festival. *Rich Relations* premiered in 1986 at The Second Stage. *1000 Airplanes on the Roof,* a collaboration with Philip Glass and designer Jerome Sirlin, toured North America, Europe, and Australia in 1988-89. *M. Butterfly* opened on Broadway in 1988 and was honored with the Tony, Drama Desk, Outer Critics Circle, and John Gassner Awards. Mr. Hwang's plays have been anthologized in *Best Plays of 1981-82, Best Short Plays of 1982, New Plays USA 1, Best Short Plays of 1985,* and *Best Plays of 1988-89.* He is the recipient of Guggenheim, Rockefeller, NEA, and NYSCA Fellowships; and serves on the board of the Theatre Communications Group. Mr. Hwang was born in 1957 of immigrant Chinese American parents; he received his undergraduate degree from Stanford University in 1979 and also attended the Yale School of Drama.

CONTENTS

INTRODUCTION

American theater is beginning to discover Americans.

Black theater, women's theater, gay theater, Asian American theater, Hispanic theater—these are more than merely fads or splinter movements. They are attempts by the American theater to come to grips with the multicultural character of our society, to portray it truthfully. As such, they represent simply the artistic face of what is essentially a political transformation.

By focusing on the smallest thing, we expose the design of the whole. If we neglect some of the communities which make up our society, our perception of the whole becomes a lie. America has traditionally denied the importance of its minorities, and this denial has been reflected in its theater, which has portrayed a relatively homogenous society, with white males as the centers and prime movers. This is ethnic theater—but the theater of only one ethnic group.

The great American temptation is to be suckered into the melting pot. We somehow believe that to be less "ethnic" is to be more human. In fact, the opposite is true: By confronting our ethnicity, we are simply confronting the roots of our humanity. The denial of this truth creates a bizarre world, cut off from the past and alienated from the present, where cosmetic surgeons offer to un-slant Asian eyes and makeup artists work to slant the eyes of Peter Ustinov, 1981's Charlie Chan.

The plays in this volume are my attempt to explore human issues without denying the color of my skin. The playwright Athol Fugard was quoted as saying, "To me, the curse of theater today is generalizing. You need a place, you need the reality first." These plays spring from the world I know best.

These plays also exist as part of the growing Asian American theater movement. Acting remains one of the professions where employment is blatently denied on the basis of race, and Asian actors who have hoped to play Shakespeare have found themselves on the outskirts of theatrical communities, forced to be mere ethnic color. Asian American theater attempts to counter this denial of our humanity. The reader who appreciates these plays, and especially those who do not, would do well to examine the work of artists such as Philip Kan Gotanda, Momoko Iko, Jessica Hagedorn, Frank Chin, Winston Tong, R.A. Shiomi, and Wakako Yamauchi, in theaters like East West Players (Los Angeles), the Asian American Theatre Company (San Francisco), Pan-Asian Repertory (New York), the Asian Multimedia Center (Seattle), and the Pacific Asian Actors Ensemble (San Diego).

Immigration is making Caucasians an increasingly smaller percentage of this country's population. This demographic trend will necessarily be reflected in the nation's artistic face, and it seems to be a healthy development. In Hawaii, for instance, where Caucasians constitute a plurality rather than a majority, a work of art is not considered somehow "less universal" because its creator is of any particular ethnic group. If this is what the future holds for American theater, we can look forward to a time when no artist will have to hide his or her face in order to work.

In 1979, I directed the first production of my first play, *FOB*, in the lounge of the Okada House dorm at Stanford University. Much has happened since then, and I am grateful to all those who have helped shape these plays, to my family and friends, from whom I am constantly stealing material, and to Joe Papp, who believed in these pieces enough to expose them to a wider audience. It is to Asian American theater people across this nation, however, that I dedicate this volume. I present these plays as an offering, with respect for the past and excitement for our future lives together.

DAVID HENRY HWANG

New York City
May, 1982

8

THE DANCE
AND THE RAILROAD

For John and Tzi

This play was commissioned by the New Federal Theater under a grant from the U.S. Department of Education. Special thanks to Jack Tchen and the New York Chinatown History Project, and Genny Chomori of the UCLA Asian American Studies Center.

The Dance and the Railroad was first produced by the Henry Street Settlement's New Federal Theater, Woodie King, Jr., and Steve Tennen, producers. It opened on March 25, 1981, with the following cast:

LONE..................................... John Lone

MA.. Tzi Ma

Alternate Actor .... Glenn Kubota

Directed by John Lone. Sculpture by Andrea Zakin, lights by Grant Ornstein, costumes by Judy Dearing; Alice Jankowiak was production stage manager; music and choreography by John Lone.

The Dance and the Railroad was then produced by Joseph Papp at the New York Shakespeare Festival Public Theater, where it opened at the Anspacher Theater on July 16, 1981, with the following cast:

LONE.....................................John Lone

MA...Tzi Ma

Alternate Actor..............................Toshi Toda

Directed by John Lone; setting by Karen Schulz; lights by Victor En Yu Tan; costumes by Judy Dearing; music and choreography by John Lone. Alice Jankowiak was production stage manager.

CHARACTERS

LONE, twenty years old, ChinaMan railroad worker.

MA, eighteen years old, ChinaMan railroad worker.

PLACE

A mountaintop near the transcontinental railroad.

TIME

June, 1867.

SYNOPSIS OF SCENES

Scene 1. Afternoon

Scene 2. Afternoon, a day later.

Scene 3. Late afternoon, four days later.

Scene 4. Late that night.

Scene 5. Just before the following dawn.

THE DANCE
AND THE RAILROAD

Scene 1

*A mountaintop. Lone is practicing opera steps. He swings his
pigtail around like a fan. Ma enters, cautiously, watches from a
hidden spot. Ma approaches Lone.*

LONE. So, there are insects hiding in the bushes.

MA. Hey, listen, we haven't met, but—

LONE. I don't spend time with insects. *(Lone whips his hair into
Ma's face; Ma backs off; Lone pursues him, swiping at Ma with his
hair.)*

MA. What the—? Cut it out! *(Ma pushes Lone away.)*

LONE. Don't push me.

MA. What was that for?

LONE. Don't ever push me again.

MA. You mess like that, you're gonna get pushed.

LONE. Don't push me.

MA. You started it. I just wanted to watch.

LONE. You "just wanted to watch." Did you ask my per-
mission?

MA. What?

LONE. Did you?

MA. C'mon.

LONE. You can't expect to get in for free.

MA. Listen. I got stuff you'll wanna hear.

LONE. You think so?

MA. Yeah. Some advice.

LONE. Advice? How old are you, anyway?

MA. Eighteen.

13

LONE. A child.

MA. Yeah. Right. a child. But listen—

20 + 10
proud

LONE. A child who tries to advise a grown man—

MA. Listen, you got this kind of attitude.

LONE. —is a child who will never grow up.

MA. You know, the ChinaMen down at camp, they can't stand it.

LONE. Oh?

MA. Yeah. You gotta watch yourself. You know what they say? They call you "Prince of the Mountain." Like you're too good to spend time with them.

LONE. Perceptive of them.

MA. After all, you never sing songs, never tell stories. They say you act like your spit is too clean for them, and they got ways to fix that.

LONE. Is that so?

MA. Like they're gonna bury you in the shit buckets, so you'll have more to clean than your nails.

LONE. But I don't shit.

MA. Or they're gonna cut out your tongue, since you never speak to them.

LONE. There's no one here worth talking to.

MA. Cut it out, Lone. Look, I'm trying to help you, all right? I got a solution.

LONE. So young yet so clever.

MA. That stuff you're doing—it's beautiful. Why don't you do it for the guys at camp? Help us celebrate?

LONE. What will "this stuff" help celebrate?

MA. C'mon. The strike, of course. Guys on a railroad gang, we gotta stick together, you know.

LONE. This is something to celebrate?

MA. Yeah. Yesterday, the weak-kneed ChinaMen, they were running around like chickens without a head: "The white devils are sending their soldiers! Shoot us all!" But now, look—day four, see? Still in one piece. Those soldiers—we've never seen a gun or a bullet.

14

LONE. So you're all warrior-spirits, huh?

MA. They're scared of us, Lone—that's what it means.

LONE. I appreciate your advice. Tell you what—you go down—

MA. Yeah?

LONE. Down to the camp—

MA. Okay.

LONE. To where the men are—

MA. Yeah?

LONE. Sit there—

MA. Yeah?

LONE. And wait for me.

MA. Okay. *(Pause.)* That's it? What do you think I am?

LONE. I think you're an insect interrupting my practice. So fly away. Go home.

MA. Look, I didn't come here to get laughed at.

LONE. No, I suppose you didn't.

MA. So just stay up here. By yourself. You deserve it.

LONE. I do.

MA. And don't expect any more help from me.

LONE. I haven't gotten any yet.

MA. If one day, you wake up and your head is buried in the shit can—

LONE. Yes?

MA. You can't find your body, your tongue is cut out—

LONE. Yes.

MA. Don't worry, 'cuz I'll be there.

LONE. Oh.

MA. To make sure your mother's head is sitting right next to yours. *(Ma exits.)*

LONE. His head is too big for this mountain. *(Returns to practicing.)*

Scene 2

Mountaintop. Next day. Lone is practicing. Ma enters.

MA. Hey.

LONE. You? Again?

MA. I forgive you.

LONE. You...what?

MA. For making fun of me yesterday. I forgive you.

LONE. You can't—

MA. No. Don't thank me.

LONE. You can't forgive me.

MA. No. Don't mention it.

LONE. You—! I never asked for your forgiveness.

MA. I know. That's just the kinda guy I am.

LONE. This is ridiculous. Why don't you leave? Go down to your friends and play soldiers, sing songs, tell stories.

MA. Ah! See? That's just it. I got other ways I wanna spend my time. Will you teach me the opera?

LONE. What?

MA. I wanna learn it. I dreamt about it all last night.

LONE. No.

MA. The dance, the opera—I can do it.

with my own get "outa here"

LONE. You think so?

MA. Yeah. When I get outa here, I wanna go back to China and perform.

LONE. You want to become an actor?

MA. Well, I wanna perform.

LONE. Don't you remember the story about the three sons whose parents send them away to learn a trade? After three years,

16

they return. The first one says, "I have become a coppersmith." The parents say, "Good. Second son, what have you become?" "I've become a silversmith." "Good—and youngest son, what about you?" "I have become an actor." When the parents hear that their son has become only an actor, they are very sad. The mother beats her head against the ground until the ground, out of pity, opens up and swallows her. The father is so angry he can't even speak, and the anger builds up inside him until it blows his body to pieces—little bits of his skin are found hanging from trees days later. You don't know how you endanger your relatives by becoming an actor.

MA. Well, I don't wanna become an "actor." That sounds terrible. I just wanna perform. Look, I'll be rich by the time I get out of here, right?

LONE. Oh?

MA. Sure. By the time I go back to China, I'll ride in gold sedan chairs, with twenty wives fanning me all around.

LONE. Twenty wives? This boy is ambitious.

MA. I'll give out pigs on New Year's and keep a stable of small birds to give to any woman who pleases me. And in my spare time, I'll perform.

LONE. Between your twenty wives and your birds, where will you find a free moment?

MA. I'll play Gwan Gung and tell stories of what life was like on the Gold Mountain.

LONE. Ma, just how long have you been in "America"?

MA. Huh? About four weeks.

LONE. You are a big dreamer.

MA. Well, all us ChinaMen here are—right? Men with little dreams—have little brains to match. They walk with their eyes down, trying to find extra grains of rice on the ground.

LONE. So, you know all about "America"? Tell me, what kind of stories will you tell?

MA. I'll say, "We laid tracks like soldiers. Mountains? We hung from cliffs in baskets and the winds blew us like birds. Snow? We lived underground like moles for days at a time. Deserts? We—"

17

LONE. Wait. Wait. How do you know these things after only four weeks?

MA. They told me—the other ChinaMen on the gang. We've been telling stories ever since the strike began.

LONE. They make it sound like it's very enjoyable.

MA. They said it is.

LONE. Oh? And you believe them?

MA. They're my friends. Living underground in winter—sounds exciting, huh?

LONE. Did they say anything about the cold?

MA. Oh, I already know about that. They told me about the mild winters and the warm snow.

LONE. Warm snow?

MA. When I go home, I'll bring some back to show my brothers.

LONE. Bring some—? On the boat?

MA. They'll be shocked—they never seen American snow before.

LONE. You can't. By the time you get snow to the boat, it'll have melted, evaporated, and returned as rain already.

MA. No.

LONE. No?

MA. Stupid.

LONE. Me?

MA. You been here awhile, haven't you?

LONE. Yes. Two years.

MA. Then how come you're so stupid? This is the Gold Mountain. The snow here doesn't melt. It's not wet.

LONE. That's what they told you?

MA. Yeah. It's true.

LONE. Did anyone show you any of this snow?

MA. No. It's not winter.

LONE. So where does it go?

MA. Huh?

LONE. Where does it go, if it doesn't melt? What happens to it?

MA. The snow? I dunno. I guess it just stays around.

LONE. So where is it? Do you see any?

MA. Here? Well, no, but... *(Pause.)* This is probably one of those places where it doesn't snow—even in winter.

LONE. Oh.

MA. Anyway, what's the use of me telling you what you already know? Hey, c'mon—teach me some of that stuff. Look—I've been practicing the walk—how's this? *(Demonstrates.)*

LONE. You look like a duck in heat.

MA. Hey—it's a start, isn't it?

LONE. Tell you what—you want to play some *die siu?*

MA. *Die siu?* Sure.

LONE. You know, I'm pretty good.

MA. Hey, I play with the guys at camp. You can't be any better than Lee—he's really got it down. *(Lone pulls out a case with two dice.)*

LONE. I used to play till morning.

MA. Hey, us too. We see the sun start to rise, and say, "Hey, if we go to sleep now, we'll never get up for work." So we just keep playing.

LONE. *(Holding out dice.) Die* or *Siu?*

MA. *Siu.*

LONE. You sure?

MA. Yeah!

LONE. All right. *(He rolls.) Die!*

MA. *Siu! (They see the result.)*

MA. Not bad. *(They continue taking turns rolling through the following section; Ma always loses.)*

LONE. I haven't touched these in two years.

MA. I gotta practice more.

LONE. Have you lost much money?

MA. Huh? So what?

LONE. Oh, you have gold hidden in all your shirt linings, huh?

MA. Here in "America"—losing is no problem. You know—End of the Year Bonus?

19

LONE. Oh, right.

MA. After I get that, I'll laugh at what I lost.

LONE. Lee told you there was a bonus, right?

MA. How'd you know?

LONE. When I arrived here, Lee told me there was a bonus, too.

MA. Lee teach you how to play?

LONE. Him? He talked to me a lot.

MA. Look, why don't you come down and start playing with the guys again?

LONE. "The guys."

MA. Before we start playing, Lee uses a stick to write "Kill!" in the dirt.

LONE. You seem to live for your nights with "the guys."

MA. What's life without friends, huh?

LONE. Well, why do *you* think I stopped playing?

MA. Hey, maybe you were the one getting killed, huh?

LONE. What?

MA. Hey, just kidding.

LONE. Who's getting killed here?

MA. Just a joke.

LONE. That's not a joke, it's blasphemy.

MA. Look, obviously you stopped playing 'cause you wanted to practice the opera.

LONE. Do you understand that discipline?

MA. But, I mean, you don't have to overdo it either. You don't have to treat 'em like dirt. I mean, who are you trying to impress?

(Pause. Lone throws dice into the bushes.)

LONE. Oooops. Better go see who won.

MA. Hey! C'mon! Help me look!

LONE. If you find them, they are yours.

MA. You serious?

LONE. Yes.

MA. Here. *(Finds the dice.)*

LONE. Who won?

MA. I didn't check.

20

LONE. Well, no matter. Keep the dice. Take them and go play with your friends.

MA. Here. *(He offers them to Lone.)* A present.

LONE. A present? This isn't a present!

MA. They're mine, aren't they? You gave them to me, right?

LONE. Well, yes, but—

MA. So now I'm giving them to you.

LONE. You can't give me a present. I don't want them.

MA. You wanted them enough to keep them two years.

LONE. I'd forgotten I had them.

MA. See, I know, Lone. You wanna get rid of me. But you can't. I'm paying for lessons.

LONE. With my dice.

MA. Mine now. *(He offers them again.)* Here. *(Pause. Lone runs Ma's hand across his forehead.)*

LONE. Feel this.

MA. Hey!

LONE. Pretty wet, huh?

MA. Big deal.

LONE. Well, its not from playing *die siu.*

MA. I know how to sweat. I wouldn't be here if I didn't.

LONE. Yes, but are you willing to sweat after you've finished sweating? Are you willing to come up after you've spent the whole day chipping half an inch off a rock, and punish your body some more?

MA. Yeah. Even after work, I still—

LONE. No, you don't. You want to gamble, and tell dirty stories, and dress up like women to do shows.

MA. Hey, I never did that.

LONE. You've only been here a month. *(Pause.)* And what about "the guys"? They're not going to treat you so well once you stop playing with them. Are you willing to work all day listening to them whisper, "That one—let's put spiders in his soup"?

MA. They won't do that to me. With you, it's different.

LONE. Is it?

MA. You don't have to act that way.

LONE. What way?

21

MA. Like you're so much better than them.

LONE. No. You haven't even begun to understand. To practice every day, you must have a fear to force you up here.

MA. A fear? No—it's 'cause what you're doing is beautiful.

LONE. No.

MA. I've seen it.

LONE. It's ugly to practice when the mountain has turned your muscles to ice. When my body hurts too much to come here, I look at the other ChinaMen and think, "They are dead. Their muscles work only because the white man forces them. I live because I can still force my muscles to work for me." Say it. "They are dead."

MA. No. They're my friends.

LONE. Well, then, take your dice down to your friends.

MA. But I want to learn—

LONE. This is your first lesson.

MA. Look, it shouldn't matter—

LONE. It does.

MA. It shouldn't matter what I think.

LONE. Attitude is everything.

MA. But as long as I come up, do the exercises—

LONE. I'm not going to waste time on a quitter.

MA. I'm not!

LONE. Then say it.—"They are dead men."

MA. I can't.

LONE. Then you will never have the dedication.

MA. That doesn't prove anything.

LONE. I will not teach a dead man.

MA. What?

LONE. If you can't see it, then you're dead too.

MA. Don't start pinning—

LONE. Say it!

MA. All right.

LONE. What?

MA. All right. I'm one of them. I'm a dead man too. *(Pause.)*

LONE. I thought as much. So, go. You have your friends.

MA. But I don't have a teacher.

LONE. I don't think you need both.

MA. Are you sure?

LONE. I'm being questioned by a child. *(Lone returns to practicing. Silence.)*

MA. Look, Lone, I'll come up here every night—after work—I'll spend my time practicing, okay? *(Pause.)* But I'm not gonna say that they're dead. Look at them. They're on strike; dead men don't go on strike, Lone. The white devils—they try and stick us with a ten-hour day. We want a return to eight hours and also a fourteen-dollar-a-month raise. I learned the demon English—listen: "Eight hour a day good for white man, alla same good for ChinaMan." These are the demands of live ChinaMen, Lone. Dead men don't complain.

LONE. All right, this is something new. But no one can judge the ChinaMen till after the strike.

MA. They say we'll hold out for months if we have to. The smart men will live on what we've hoarded.

LONE. A ChinaMan's mouth can swallow the earth. *(He takes the dice.)* While the strike is on, I'll teach you.

MA. And afterwards?

LONE. Afterwards—we'll decide then whether these are dead or live men.

MA. When can we start?

LONE. We've already begun. Give me your hand.

Scene 3

Lone and Ma are doing physical exercises.

MA. How long will it be before I can play Gwan Gung?

LONE. How long before a dog can play the violin?

MA. Old Ah Hong—have you heard him play the violin?

LONE. Yes. Now, he should take his violin and give it to a dog.

MA. I think he sounds okay.

LONE. I think he caused that avalanche last winter.

MA. He used to play for weddings back home.

LONE. Ah Hong?

MA. That's what he said.

LONE. You probably heard wrong.

MA. No.

LONE. He probably said he played for funerals.

MA. He's been playing for the guys down at camp.

LONE. He should play for the white devils—that will end this stupid strike.

MA. Yang told me for sure—it'll be over by tomorrow.

LONE. Eight days already. And Yang doesn't know anything.

MA. He said they're already down to an eight-hour and five dollar raise at the bargaining sessions.

LONE. Yang eats too much opium.

MA. That doesn't mean he's wrong about this.

LONE. You can't trust him. One time—last year—he went around camp looking in everybody's eyes and saying, "Your nails are too long. They're hurting my eyes." This went on for a week. Finally, all the men clipped their nails, made a big pile, which they wrapped in leaves and gave to him. Yang used the nails to season his food—he put it in his soup, sprinkled it on his rice, and never said a word about it again. Now tell me—are you going to trust a man who eats other men's fingernails?

MA. Well, all I know is we won't go back to work until they meet all our demands. Listen, teach me some Gwan Gung steps.

LONE. I should have expected this. A boy who wants to have twenty wives is the type who demands more than he can handle.

MA. Just a few.

LONE. It takes years before an actor can play Gwan Gung.

MA. I can do it. I spend a lot of time watching the opera when it comes around. Every time I see Gwan Gung, I say, "Yeah. That's me. The god of fighters. The god of adventurers. We have the same kind of spirit."

LONE. I tell you, if you work very hard, when you return to China, you can perhaps be the Second Clown.

MA. Second Clown?

LONE. If you work hard.

MA. What's the Second Clown?

LONE. You can play the *p'ip'a,* and dance and jump all over.

MA. I'll buy them.

LONE. Excuse me?

MA. I'm going to be rich, remember? I'll buy a troupe and force them to let me play Gwan Gung.

LONE. I hope you have enough money, then, to pay audiences to sit through your show.

MA. You mean, I'm going to have to practice here every night— and in return, all I can play is the Second Clown?

LONE. If you work hard.

MA. Am I that bad? Maybe I shouldn't even try to do this. Maybe I should just go down.

LONE. It's not you. Everyone must earn the right to play Gwan Gung. I entered opera school when I was ten years old. My parents decided to sell me for ten years to this opera company. I lived with eighty other boys and we slept in bunks four beds high and hid our candy and rice cakes from each other. After eight years, I was studying to play Gwan Gung.

MA. Eight years?

LONE. I was one of the best in my class. One day, I was summoned by my master, who told me I was to go home for two days, because my mother had fallen very ill and was dying. When I arrived home, Mother was standing at the door waiting, not sick at all. Her first words to me, the son away for eight years, were, "You've been playing while your village has starved. You must go to the Gold Mountain and work."

MA. And you never returned to school?

LONE. I went from a room with eighty boys to a ship with three hundred men. So, you see, it does not come easily to play Gwan Gung?

MA. Did you want to play Gwan Gung?

LONE. What a foolish question!

MA. Well, you're better off this way.

LONE. What?

MA. Actors—they don't make much money. Here, you make a bundle, then go back and be an actor again. Best of both worlds.

LONE. "Best of both worlds."

MA. Yeah! *(Lone drops to the ground, begins imitating a duck, waddling and quacking.)*

MA. Lone? What are you doing? *(Lone quacks.)* You're a duck? *(Lone quacks.)* I can see that. *(Lone quacks.)* Is this an exercise? Am I supposed to do this? *(Lone quacks.)* This is dumb. I never seen Gwan Gung waddle. *(Lone quacks.)* Okay. All right. I'll do it. *(Ma and Lone quack and waddle.)* You know, I never realized before how uncomfortable a duck's life is. And you have to listen to yourself quacking all day. Go crazy! *(Lone stands up straight.)* Now, what was that all about?

LONE. No, no. Stay down there, duck.

MA. What's the—

LONE. *(Prompting.)* Quack, quack, quack.

MA. I don't—

LONE. Act your species!

MA. I'm not a duck!

LONE. Nothing worse than a duck that doesn't know his place.

MA. All right. *(Mechanically.)* Quack, quack.

LONE. More.

MA. Quack.

LONE. More!

MA. Quack, quack, quack! *(Ma now continues quacking, as Lone gives commands.)*

LONE. Louder! It's your mating call! Think of your twenty duck wives! Good! Louder! Project! More! Don't slow down! Put your tail feathers into it! They can't hear you! *(Ma is now quacking up a storm. Lone exits, unnoticed by Ma.)*

MA. Quack! Quack! Quack! Quack. Quack...quack. *(He looks*

around.) Quack...quack...Lone?...Lone? *(He waddles around the stage looking.)* Lone, where are you? Where'd you go? *(He stops, scratches his left leg with his right foot.)* C'mon—stop playing around. What is this? *(Lone enters as a tiger, unseen by Ma.)* Look, let's call it a day, okay? I'm getting hungry. *(Ma turns around, notices Lone right before Lone is to bite him.)* Aaaaah! Quack, quack, quack! *(They face off, in character as animals. Duck-Ma is terrified.)*

LONE. Grrrr!

MA. *(As a cry for help.)* Quack, quack, quack! *(Lone pounces on Ma. They struggle, in character. Ma is quacking madly, eyes tightly closed. Lone stands up striaght. Ma continues to quack.)*

LONE. Stand up.

MA. *(Eyes still closed.)* Quack, quack, quack!

LONE. *(Louder.)* Stand up!

MA. *(Opening his eyes.)* Oh.

LONE. What are you?

MA. Huh?

LONE. A ChinaMan or a duck?

MA. Huh? Gimme a second to remember.

LONE. You like being a duck?

MA. My feet fell asleep.

LONE. You change forms so easily.

MA. You said to.

LONE. What else could you turn into?

MA. Well, you scared me—sneaking up like that.

LONE. Perhaps a rock. That would be useful. When the men need to rest, they can sit on you.

MA. I got carried away.

LONE. Let's try...a locust. Can you become a locust?

MA. No. Let's cut this, okay?

LONE. Here. It's easy. You just have to know how to hop.

MA. You're not gonna get me—

LONE. Like this. *(He demonstrates.)*

MA. Forget it, Lone.

LONE. I'm a locust. *(He begins jumping toward Ma.)*

MA. Hey! Get away!

LONE. I devour whole fields.

MA. Stop it.

LONE. I starve babies before they are born.

MA. Hey, look, stop it!

LONE. I cause famines and destroy villages.

MA. I'm warning you! Get away!

LONE. What are you going to do? You can't kill a locust.

MA. You're not a locust.

LONE. You kill one, and another sits on your hand.

MA. Stop following me.

LONE. Locusts always trouble people. If not, we'd feel useless. Now, if you became a locust, too...

MA. I'm not going to become a locust.

LONE. Just stick your teeth out!

MA. I'm not gonna be a bug! It's stupid!

LONE. No man who's just been a duck has the right to call anything stupid.

MA. I thought you were trying to teach me something.

LONE. I am. Go ahead.

MA. All right. There. That look right?

LONE. Your legs should be a little lower. Lower! There. That's adequate. So, how does it feel to be a locust? *(Lone gets up.)*

MA. I dunno. How long do I have to do this?

LONE. Could you do it for three years?

MA. Three years? Don't be—

LONE. You couldn't, could you? Could you be a duck for that long?

MA. Look, I wasn't born to be either of those.

LONE. Exactly. Well, I wasn't born to work on a railroad, either. "Best of both worlds." How can you be such an insect! *(Pause.)*

MA. Lone...

LONE. Stay down there! Don't move! I've never told anyone my story—the story of my parents' kidnapping me from school. All the time we were crossing the ocean, the last two years here—I've kept my mouth shut. To you, I finally tell it. And all you can say is,

"Best of both worlds." You're a bug to me, a locust. You think you understand the dedication one must have to be in the opera? You think it's the same as working on a railroad.

MA. Lone, all I was saying is that you'll go back too, and—

LONE. You're no longer a student of mine.

MA. What?

LONE. You have no dedication.

MA. Lone, I'm sorry.

LONE. Get up.

MA. I'm honored that you told me that.

LONE. Get up.

MA. No.

LONE. No?

MA. I don't want to. I want to talk.

LONE. Well, I've learned from the past. You're stubborn. You don't go. All right. Stay there. If you want to prove to me that you're dedicated, be a locust till morning. I'll go.

MA. Lone, I'm really honored that you told me.

LONE. I'll return in the morning. *(Exits.)*

MA. Lone? Lone, that's ridiculous. You think I'm gonna stay like this? If you do, you're crazy. Lone? Come back here.

Scene 4

Night. Ma, alone, as a locust.

MA. Locusts travel in huge swarms, so large that when they cross the sky, they block out the sun, like a storm. Second Uncle—back home—when he was a young man, his whole crop got wiped out by locusts one year. In the famine that followed, Second Uncle lost his eldest son and his second wife—the one he married for love. Even to this day, we look around before saying the word "locust," to make sure Second Uncle is out of hearing range. About eight years ago, my brother and I discovered Second Uncle's cave in back of the stream near our house. We saw him come out of it one day around noon. Later, just before the sun went down, we sneaked in. We only looked once. Inside, there must have been hundreds— maybe five hundred or more—grasshoppers in huge bamboo cages—and around them—stacks of grasshopper legs, grasshoppers with one leg, still trying to hop but toppling like trees coughing, grasshoppers wrapped around sharp branches rolling from side to side, grasshopper legs cut off grasshopper bodies, then tied around grasshoppers and tightened till grasshoppers died. Every conceivable stage of life and death, subject to every conceivable grasshopper torture. We ran out quickly, my brother and I—we knew an evil place by the thickness of the air. Now, I think of Second Uncle. How sad that the locusts forced him to take out his agony on innocent grasshoppers. What if Second Uncle could see me now? Would he cut off my legs? He might as well. I can barely feel them. But then again, Second Uncle never tortured actual locusts, just weak grasshoppers.

Scene 5

Night. Ma still as a locust.

LONE. *(Off, singing.)*
Hit your hardest
Pound out your tears
The more you try
The more you'll cry
At how little I've moved
And how large I loom
By the time the sun goes down
MA. You look rested.
LONE. Me?

30

MA. Well, you sound rested.

LONE. No, not at all.

MA. Maybe I'm just comparing you to me.

LONE. I didn't even close my eyes all last night.

MA. Aw, Lone, you didn't have to stay up for me. You coulda just come up here and—

LONE. For you?

MA. —apologized and everything woulda been—

LONE. I didn't stay up for you.

MA. Huh? You didn't?

LONE. No.

MA. Oh. You sure?

LONE. Positive. I was thinking, that's all.

MA. About me?

LONE. Well...

MA. Even a little?

LONE. I was thinking about the ChinaMen—and you. Get up, Ma.

MA. Aw, do I have to? I've gotten to know these grasshoppers real well.

LONE. Get up. I have a lot to tell you.

MA. What'll they think? They take me in, even though I'm a little large, then they find out I'm a human being. I stepped on their kids. No trust. Gimme a hand, will you? *(Lone helps Ma up, but Ma's legs can't support him.)* Aw, shit. My legs are coming off. *(He lies down and tries to straighten them out.)*

LONE. I have many surprises. First, you will play Gwan Gung.

MA. My legs will be sent home without me. What'll my family think? Come to port to meet me and all they get is two legs.

LONE. Did you hear me?

MA. Hold on. I can't be in agony and listen to Chinese at the same time.

LONE. Did you hear my first surprise?

MA. No. I'm too busy screaming.

LONE. I said, you'll play Gwan Gung.

31

MA. Gwan Gung?

LONE. Yes.

MA. Me?

LONE. Yes.

MA. Without legs?

LONE. What?

MA. That might be good.

LONE. Stop that!

MA. I'll become a legend. Like the blind man who defended Amoy.

LONE. Did you hear?

MA. "The legless man who played Gwan Gung."

LONE. Isn't this what you want? To play Gwan Gung?

MA. No, I just wanna sleep.

LONE. No, you don't. Look. Here. I brought you something.

MA. Food?

LONE. Here. Some rice.

MA. Thanks, Lone. And duck?

LONE. Just a little.

MA. Where'd you get the duck?

LONE. Just bones and skin.

MA. We don't have duck. And the white devils have been blockading the food.

LONE. Sing—he had some left over.

MA. Sing? That thief?

LONE. And something to go with it.

MA. What? Lone, where did you find whiskey?

LONE. You know, Sing—he has almost anything.

MA. Yeah. For a price.

LONE. Once, even some thousand-day-old eggs.

MA. He's a thief. That's what they told me.

LONE. Not if you're his friend.

MA. Sing don't have any real friends. Everyone talks about him bein' tied in to the head of the klan in San Francisco. Lone, you didn't have to do this. Here. Have some.

LONE. I had plenty.

32

MA. Don't gimme that. This cost you plenty, Lone.

LONE. Well, I thought if we were going to celebrate, we should do it as well as we would at home.

MA. Celebrate? What for? Wait.

LONE. Ma, the strike is over.

MA. Shit, I knew it. And we won, right?

LONE. Yes, the ChinaMen have won. They can do more than just talk.

MA. I told you. Didn't I tell you?

LONE. Yes. Yes, you did.

MA. Yang told me it was gonna be done. He said—

LONE. Yes, I remember.

MA. Didn't I tell you? Huh?

LONE. Ma, eat your duck.

MA. Nine days. In nine days, we civilized the white devils. I knew it. I knew we'd hold out till their ears started twitching. So that's where you got the duck, right? At the celebration?

LONE. No, there wasn't a celebration.

MA. Huh? You sure? ChinaMen—they look for any excuse to party.

LONE. But I thought *we* should celebrate.

MA. Well, that's for sure.

LONE. So you will play Gwan Gung.

MA. God, nine days. Shit, it's finally done. Well, we'll show them how to party. Make noise. Jump off rocks. Make the mountain shake.

LONE. We'll wash your body, to prepare you for the role.

MA. What role?

LONE. Gwan Gung. I've been telling you.

MA. I don't wanna play Gwan Gung.

LONE. You've shown the dedication required to become my student, so—

MA. Lone, you think I stayed up last night 'cause I wanted to play Gwan Gung?

LONE. You said you were like him.

MA. I am. Gwan Gung stayed up all night once to prove his loyalty.

33

Well, now I have too. Lone, I'm honored that you told me your story.

LONE. Yes...That is like Gwan Gung.

MA. Good. So let's do an opera about *me*.

LONE. What?

MA. You wanna party or what?

LONE. About you?

MA. You said I was like Gwan Gung, didn't you?

LONE. Yes, but—

MA. Well, look at the operas he's got. I ain't even got one.

LONE. Still, you can't—

MA. You tell me, is that fair?

LONE. You can't do an opera about yourself.

MA. I just won a victory, didn't I. I deserve an opera in my honor.

LONE. But it's not traditional.

MA. Traditional? Lone, you gotta figure any way I could do Gwan Gung wasn't gonna be traditional anyway. I may be as good a guy as him, but he's a better dancer. *(Sings.)*

Old Gwan Gung, just sits about

Till the dime-store fighters have had it out

Then he pitches his peach pit

Combs his beard

Draws his sword

And they scatter in fear

LONE. What are you talking about?

MA. I just won a great victory. I get—whatcha call it?—poetic license. C'mon. Hit the gongs. I'll immortalize my story.

LONE. I refuse. This goes against all my training. I try and give you your wish and—

MA. Do it. Gimme my wish. Hit the gongs.

LONE. I never—I can't.

MA. Can't what? Don't think I'm worth an opera? No, I guess not. I forgot—you think I'm just one of those dead men. *(Silence. Lone pulls out a gong. Ma gets into position. Lone hits the gong. They do the following in a mock-Chinese-opera style.)* I am Me. Yesterday, I was kicked out of my house by my three elder brothers, calling me the lazy dreamer of the family. I am sitting here in front of the temple trying to decide how I will avenge this indignity. Here comes the poorest beggar in this village. *(He cues Lone.)* He is called Fleaman because his body is the most popular meeting place for fleas from around the province.

LONE. *(Singing.)*
Fleas in love,
Find your happiness
In the gray scraps of my suit

MA. Hello, Flea—

LONE. *(Continuing.)*
Fleas in need,
Shield your families
In the gray hairs of my beard

MA. Hello, Flea— *(Lone cuts Ma off, continues an extended improvised aria.)* Hello, Fleaman.

LONE. Hello, Ma. Are you interested in providing a home for these fleas?

MA. No!

LONE. This couple here—seeking to start a new home. Housing today is so hard to find. How about your left arm?

MA. I may have plenty of my own fleas in time. I have been thrown out by my elder brothers.

LONE. Are you seeking revenge? A flea epidemic on your house? *(To a flea.)* Get back there. You should be asleep. Your mother will worry.

MA. Nothing would make my brothers angrier than seeing me rich.

LONE. Rich? After the bad crops of the last three years, even the fleas are thinking of moving north.

MA. I heard a white devil talk yesterday.

LONE. Oh—with hair the color of a sick chicken and eyes round as eggs? The fleas and I call him Chicken-Laying-an-Egg.

MA. He said we can make our fortunes on the Gold Mountain, where work is play and the sun scares off snow.

35

LONE. Don't listen to chicken-brains.

MA. Why not? He said gold grows like weeds.

LONE. I have heard that it is slavery.

MA. Slavery? What do you know, Fleaman? Who told you? The fleas? Yes, I will go to Gold Mountain. *(Gongs. Ma strikes a submissive pose to Lone.)*

LONE. "The one hundred twenty-five dollars passage money is to be paid to the said head of said Hong, who will make arrangements with the coolies, that their wages shall be deducted until the debt is absorbed." *(Ma bows to Lone. Gongs. They pick up fighting sticks and do a water-crossing dance. Dance ends. They stoop next to each other and rock.)*

MA. I have been in the bottom of this boat for thirty-six days now. Tang, how many have died?

LONE. Not me. I'll live through this ride.

MA. I didn't ask how you are.

LONE. But why's the Gold Mountain so far?

MA. We left with three hundred and three.

LONE. My family's depending on me.

MA. So tell me, how many have died?

LONE. I'll be the last one alive.

MA. That's not what I wanted to know.

LONE. I'll find some fresh air in this hole.

MA. I asked, how many have died.

LONE. Is that a crack in the side?

MA. Are you listening to me?

LONE. If I had some air—

MA. I asked, don't you see—?

LONE. The crack—over there—

MA. Will you answer me, please?

LONE. I need to get out.

MA. The rest here agree—

LONE. I can't stand the smell.

MA. That a hundred eighty—

LONE. I can't see the air—

MA. Of us will not see—

36

LONE. And I can't die.

MA. Our Gold Mountain dream. *(Lone/Tang dies; Ma throws his body overboard. The boat docks. Ma exits, walks through the streets. He picks up one of the fighting sticks, while Lone becomes the mountain.)* I have been given my pickax. Now I will attack the mountain. *(Ma does a dance of labor. Lone sings.)*

LONE.

Hit your hardest

Pound out your tears

The more you try

The more you'll cry

At how little I've moved

And how large I loom

By the time the sun goes down

(Dance stops.)

MA. This mountain is clever. But why shouldn't it be? It's fighting for its life, like we fight for ours. *(The mountain picks up a stick. Ma and the mountain do a battle dance. Dance ends.)* This mountain not only defends itself—it also attacks. It turns our strength against us. *(Lone does Ma's labor dance, while Ma plants explosives in midair. Dance ends.)* This mountian has survived for millions of years. Its wisdom is immense. *(Lone and Ma begin a second battle dance. This one ends with them working the battle sticks together. Lone breaks away, does a warrior strut.)*

LONE. I am a white devil! Listen to my stupid language: "Wha che doo doo blah blah." Look at my wide eyes—like I have drunk seventy-two pots of tea. Look at my funny hair—twisting, turning, like a snake telling lies. *(To Ma.)* Bla bla doo doo tee tee.

MA. We don't understand English.

LONE. *(Angry.)* Bla bla doo doo tee tee!

MA. *(With Chinese accent.)* Please you-ah speak-ah Chinese?

LONE. Oh. Work—uh—one—two—more—work—two—

MA. Two hours more? Stupid demons. As confused as your hair. We will strike! *(Gongs. Ma is on strike.)*

MA. *(In broken English.)* Eight hours day good for white man, alla same food for ChinaMan.

LONE. The strike is over! We've won!

MA. I knew we would.

LONE. We forced the white devil to act civilized.

MA. Tamed the barbarians!

LONE. Did you think—

MA. Who woulda thought?

LONE. —it could be done?

MA. Who?

LONE. But who?

MA. Who could tame them?

MA. and LONE. Only a ChinaMan! *(They laugh.)*

LONE. Well, c'mon.

MA. Let's celebrate!

LONE. We have.

MA. Oh.

LONE. Back to work.

MA. But we've won the strike.

LONE. I know. Congratulations! And now—

MA. —back to work?

LONE. Right.

MA. No.

LONE. But the strike is over. *(Lone tosses Ma a stick. They resume their stick battle as before, but Ma is heard over Lone's singing.)*

LONE.	MA.
Hit your hardest	Wait.
Pound out your tears	I'm tired of this!
The more you try	How do we end it?
The more you'll cry	Let's stop now, all right?
At how little I've moved	Look, I said enough!
And how large I loom	
By the time the sun goes	
down	

(Ma tosses his stick away, but Lone is already aiming a blow toward it, so that Lone hits Ma instead and knocks him down.)

MA. Oh! Shit...

LONE. I'm sorry! Are you all right?

MA. Yeah. I guess.

LONE. Why'd you let go? You can't just do that.

MA. I'm bleeding.

LONE. That was stupid—where?

MA. Here.

LONE. No.

MA. Ow!

LONE. There will probably be a bump.

MA. I dunno.

LONE. What?

MA. I dunno why I let go.

LONE. It was stupid.

MA. But how were we going to end the opera?

LONE. Here. *(He applies whiskey to Ma's bruise.)* I don't know.

MA. Why didn't we just end it with the celebration? Ow! Careful.

LONE. Sorry. But Ma, the celebration's not the end. We're returning to work. Today. At dawn.

MA. What?

LONE. We've already lost nine days of work. But we got eight hours.

MA. Today? That's terrible.

LONE. What do you think we're here for? But they listened to our demands. We're getting a raise.

MA. Fourteen dollars.

LONE. No. Eight.

MA. What?

LONE. We had to compromise. We got an eight-dollar raise.

MA. But we wanted fourteen. Why didn't we get fourteen?

LONE. It was the best deal they could get. Congratulations.

MA. Congratulations? Look, Lone, I'm sick of you making fun of the ChinaMen.

LONE. Ma, I'm not. For the first time. I was wrong. We got eight dollars.

MA. We wanted fourteen.

LONE. But we got eight hours.

MA. We'll go back on strike.

LONE. Why?

MA. We could hold out for months.

LONE. And lose all that work?

MA. But we gave in.

LONE. You're being ridiculous. We got eight hours. Besides, it's already been decided.

MA. I didn't decide. I wasn't there. You made me stay up here.

LONE. The heads of the gangs decide.

MA. And that's it?

LONE. It's done.

MA. Back to work? That's what they decided? Lone, I don't want to go back to work.

LONE. Who does?

MA. I forgot what it's like.

LONE. You'll pick up the technique again soon enough.

MA. I mean, what it's like to have them telling you what to do all the time. Using up your strength.

LONE. I thought you said even after work, you still feel good.

MA. Some days. But others... *(Pause.)* I get so frustrated sometimes. At the rock. The rock doesn't give in. It's not human. I wanna claw it with my fingers, but that would just rip them up. I wanna throw myself head first onto it, but it'd just knock my skull open. The rock would knock my skull open, then just sit there, still like nothing had happened, like a faceless Buddha. *(Pause.)* Lone, when do I get out of here?

LONE. Well, the railroad may get finished—

MA. It'll never get finished.

LONE. —or you may get rich.

MA. Rich. Right. This is the Gold Mountain. *(Pause.)* Lone, has anyone ever gone home rich from here?

LONE. Yes. Some.

MA. But most?

LONE. Most ... do go home.

MA. Do you still have the fear?

LONE. The fear?

MA. That you'll become like them—dead men?

LONE. Maybe I was wrong about them.

MA. Well, I do. You wanted me to say it before. I can say it now: "They are dead men." Their greatest accomplishment was to win a strike that's gotten us nothing.

LONE. They're sending money home.

MA. No.

LONE. It's not much, I know, but it's something.

MA. Lone, I'm not even doing that. If I don't get rich here, I might as well die here. Let my brothers laugh in peace.

LONE. Ma, you're too soft to get rich here, naive—you believed the snow was warm.

MA. I've got to change myself. Toughen up. Take no shit. Count my change. Learn to gamble. Learn to win. Learn to stare. Learn to deny. Learn to look at men with opaque eyes.

LONE. You want to do that?

MA. I will. 'Cause I've got the fear. You've given it to me. *(Pause.)*

LONE. Will I see you here tonight?

MA. Tonight?

LONE. I just thought I'd ask.

MA. I'm sorry, Lone. I haven't got time to be the Second Clown.

LONE. I thought you might not.

MA. Sorry.

LONE. You could have been a ... fair actor.

MA. You coming down? I gotta get ready for work. This is gonna be a terrible day. My legs are sore and my arms are outa practice.

LONE. You go first. I'm going to practice some before work. There's still time.

MA. Practice? But you said you lost your fear. And you said that's what brings you up here.

LONE. I guess I was wrong about that, too. Today I am dancing for no reason at all.

MA. Do whatever you want. See you down at camp.

LONE. Could you do me a favor?

MA. A favor?

LONE. Could you take this down so I don't have to take it all? *(Lone points to a pile of props.)*

MA. Well, okay. *(Pause.)* But this is the last time.

LONE. Of course, Ma. *(Ma exits.)* See you soon. The last time. I suppose so. *(Lone resumes practicing. He twirls his hair around as in the beginning of the play. The sun begins to rise. It continues rising until Lone is moving and seen only in shadow.)*

CURTAIN

PROPERTY LIST

Case with two dice
Gong
Fighting sticks (2)
Bottle of whiskey

FAMILY DEVOTIONS

*For my Ama and Ankong,
and Sam Shepard*

Family Devotions was produced by Joseph Papp at the New York Shakespeare Festival Public Theater, where it opened in the Newman Theater on October 18, 1981, with the following cast:

JOANNE.....................................Jodi Long

WILBUR ....Jim Ishida

JENNY ....Lauren Tom

AMA.......................................Tina Chen

POPO.......................................June Kim

HANNAH................................Helen Funai

ROBERT..........................Michael Paul Chan

DI-GOU ....Victor Wong

CHESTER ....Marc Hayashi

Directed by Robert Alan Ackerman. Settings by David Gropman. Lights by Tom Skelton. Costumes by Willa Kim.

CHARACTERS

JOANNE, late thirties, Chinese American raised in the Philippines.

WILBUR, her husband, Japanese American, nisei (second generation).

JENNY, their daughter, seventeen.

AMA, Joanne's mother, born in China, emigrated to the Philippines, then to America.

POPO, Ama's younger sister.

HANNAH, Popo's daughter and Joanne's cousin, slightly older than Joanne.

ROBERT, Hannah's husband, Chinese American, first generation.

DI-GOU, Ama and Popo's younger brother, born and raised in China, still a resident of the People's Republic of China (P.R.C.).

CHESTER, Hannah and Robert's son, early twenties.

SYNOPSIS OF SCENES

ACT I. Late afternoon, the lanai/sunroom and tennis court of a home in Bel Air, California.

ACT II. Same scene, immediately following.

DEFINITION

Jok is a Chinese rice porridge.

FAMILY DEVOTIONS

ACT I

The sunroom and backyard of a home in Bel Air. Everywhere is glass—glass roof, glass walls. Upstage of the lanai/sunroom is a patio with a barbecue and a tennis court. The tennis court leads offstage. As the curtain rises, we see a single spotlight on an old Chinese face and hear Chinese music or chanting. Suddenly, the music becomes modern-day funk or rock 'n' roll, and the lights come up to reveal the set.

The face is that of Di-gou, an older Chinese man wearing a blue suit and carrying an old suitcase. He is peering into the sunroom from the tennis court, through the glass walls. Behind him, a stream of black smoke is coming from the barbecue.

JOANNE. *(Offstage.)* Wilbur! Wilbur!
(Di-gou exits off the tennis court. Enter Joanne, from the house. She is a Chinese American woman, attractive, in her mid-thirties. She sees the smoke coming from the barbecue.) Aiii-ya! *(She heads for the barbecue, and on her way notices that the sunroom is a mess.)* Jenny! *(She runs out to the barbecue, opens it up. Billows of black smoke continue to pour out.)* Oh, gosh. Oh, golly. *(To offstage.)* Wilbur! *(She begins pulling burnt objects out of the barbecue.)* Sheee! *(She pulls out a chicken, dumps it onto the ground.)* Wilbur! *(She pulls out another chicken, does the same.)* Wilbur, the heat was too high on the barbeque! *(She begins pulling out burnt objects and tossing them all over the tennis court.)* You should have been watching it! It could have exploded! We could all have been blown up! *(She picks up another chicken, examines it.)* You think we can have some of this? *(She pauses, tosses it onto the court.)* We'll get some more chickens. We'll put barbeque sauce on them and stick them into the microwave. *(She exits into the house holding a*

chicken on the end of her fork.) Is this okay, do you think? *(Wlbur appears on the tennis court. He is a Japanese American man, nisei, in his late thirties. His hair is permed. He wears tennis clothes.)*

WILBUR. Hon? *(He looks around.)* What's up? *(He picks a burnt chicken off the tennis court.)* Hon? *(He walks over to the barbecue.)* Who—? Why's the heat off? *(He walks around the tennis court picking up chickens.)* Jesus! *(He smears grease on his white tennis shirt, notices it.)* Aw shit! *(He dumps all the chickens except one, which he has forgotten to pick up, back into the barbecue. He walks into the sunroom, gets some ice, and tries to dab at the stain.)* Hon? Will you come here a sec? *(He exits into the house. Jenny appears on the tennis court. She is seventeen. Wilbur and Joanne's daughter. She carries a large wire-mesh box.)*

JENNY. Chickie! *(Looking around.)* Chickie? Chickie, where the hell did you go? You know, it's embarrassing. It's embarrassing being this old and still having to chase a chicken all over the house. *(She sees the lone burnt chicken on the court. She creeps over slowly, then picks it up.)* Blaagh! Who cooked this? See, Chickie, this is what happens—what happens when you're a bad chickie. *(Chester, a young Chinese American male in his early twenties, appears on the tennis court. He tries to sneak up on Jenny. Jenny, to chicken.)* Look, if you bother Popo and Ama, I'm gonna catch shit, and you know what that means for you—chicken soccer. You'll be sorry if you mess with me. *(She turns around, catching Chester.)* Oh, good. You have to be here, too.

CHESTER. No, I don't. I've gotta pack.

JENNY. They'll expect you to be here when that Chinese guy gets here. What's his name? Dargwo?

CHESTER. I dunno. Dah-gim?

JENNY. Doo-goo? Something.

CHESTER. Yeah. I'm not staying.

JENNY. So what else is new?

CHESTER. I don't have time.

JENNY. You luck out 'cause you don't live here. Me—there's no way I can get away. When you leaving?

CHESTER. Tomorrow.

JENNY. Tomorrow? And you're not packed?

CHESTER. Don't rub it in. Listen, you still have my green suitcase?

JENNY. Yeah. I wish *I* had an excuse not to be here? All I need is to meet another old relative. Another goon.

CHESTER. Yeah. Where's my suitcase?

JENNY. First you have to help me find Chickie.

CHESTER. Jesus!

AMA. *(Offstage.)* Joannie!

CHESTER. *(To Jenny.)* All right. I don't want them to know I'm here. *(Chester and Jenny exit. Popo and Ama enter. They are Joanne's aunt and mother, respectively.)*

AMA. Joanne! Joanne! Jenny! Where is Joanne?

POPO. Probably busy.

AMA. Where is Jenny? Joanne?

POPO. Perhaps you can find, ah, Wilbur.

AMA. Joanne!

POPO. Ah, you never wish to see Wilbur.

AMA. I see him at wedding. That is enough. He was not at church again today.

POPO. Ah?

AMA. He will be bad influence when Di-gou arrive. Wilbur—holy spirit is not in him.

POPO. Not matter. He can perhaps eat in kitchen.

AMA. Outside!

POPO. This is his house.

AMA. All heart must join as one—

POPO. He may eat inside!

AMA. —only then, miracles can take place.

POPO. But in kitchen.

AMA. Wilbur—he never like family devotions.

POPO. Wilbur does not come from Christian family.

AMA. He come from Japanese family.

POPO. I mean to say, we—ah—very fortunate. Mama teach us all Christianity. Not like Wilbur family.

AMA. When Di-gou arrive, we will remind him. What Mama tells us.

POPO. Di-gou can remember himself.

AMA. No.

POPO. But we remember.

AMA. You forget—Di-gou, he lives in China.

POPO. So?

AMA. Torture. Communists. Make him work in rice fields.

POPO. I no longer think so.

AMA. In rice field, all the people wear wires in their heads—yes! Wires force them work all day and sing Communist song. Like this! *(She mimes harvesting rice and singing.)*

POPO. No such thing!

AMA. Yes! You remember Twa-Ling? Before we leave China, before Communist come, she say, "I will send you a picture. If Communists are good, I will stand—if bad, I will sit."

POPO. That does not mean anything!

AMA. In picture she sent, she was lying down!

POPO. Picture was not sent for ten years. Probably she forget.

AMA. You wait till Di-gou arrive. You will see.

POPO. See what?

AMA. Brainwash! You watch for little bit of wires in his hair. *(Popo notices the lone burnt chicken on the tennis court.)*

POPO. What's there?

AMA. Where?

POPO. There—on cement.

AMA. Cannot see well.

POPO. There. Black.

AMA. Oh. I see.

POPO. Looks like *gao sai.*

AMA. They sometimes have problem with the dog.

POPO. Ha!

AMA. Very bad dog.

POPO. At home, dog do that?—we shoot him.

AMA. Should be punish.

POPO. Shot! *(Pause.)* That no *gao sai.*

AMA. No? What then?

POPO. I don't know.

AMA. Oh, I know.

POPO. What?

AMA. That is Chickie.

POPO. No. That no Chickie.

AMA. They have a chicken—"Chickie." *(They get up, head toward the chicken.)*

POPO. No. That one, does not move.

AMA. Maybe sick. *(They reach the chicken.)* Aiii-ya! What happen to Chickie!

POPO. *(Picking it up.)* This chicken very sick! *(She laughs.)*

AMA. Wilbur.

POPO. Huh?

AMA. Wilbur—his temper is very bad.

POPO. No!

AMA. Yes. Perhaps Chickie bother him too much.

POPO. No—this is only a chicken.

AMA. "Chickie" *is* chicken!

POPO. No—this—another chicken.

AMA. How you know?

POPO. No matter now. Like this, all chicken look same. Here. Throw away. No good.

AMA. Very bad temper. Japanese man. *(Ama sees Popo looking for a trash can.)* Wait.

POPO. Huh?

AMA. Jenny—might want to keep it.

POPO. This?

AMA. Leave here until we know. *(She takes the chicken from Popo.)*

POPO. No, throw away. *(She takes it back.)* Stink up whole place soon.

AMA. Don't want to anger Wilbur!

POPO. You pig-head!

AMA. He do this to Chickie—think what he will do to us?

POPO. *Zin gao tza!* [Always so much trouble!]

AMA. You don't know Japanese man! *(Ama knocks the chicken from Popo's hands; they circle around it like boxers sparring.)*

POPO. *Pah-di!* [Spank you!]

AMA. Remember? During war? Pictures they show us? Always—Japanese man kill Chinese!

POPO. Go away, pig-head!

AMA. In picture—Japanese always kill and laugh, kill and laugh.

POPO. If dirty, should throw away!

AMA. Sometimes—torture and laugh, too.

POPO. Wilbur not like that! Hardly even laugh!

AMA. When he kill Chickie, then he laugh! *(They both grab the chicken; Joanne enters, sees them.)*

JOANNE. Hi, Mom, Auntie. Who cleaned up the chicken?

AMA. Huh? This is not Chickie?

POPO. *(To Ama.)* Tell you things, you never listen. *(Gong-gong-ah!* [Idiot!]

JOANNE. When's Hannah getting here?

POPO. Hannah—she is at airport.

JOANNE. We had a little accident and I need help programming the microwave. Last time, I put a roast inside and it disintegrated. She should be here already.

AMA. Joanne, you prepare for family devotions?

JOANNE. Of course, Mom. I had the maid set up everything just like you said. *(She exits.)*

AMA. Good. Praise to God will bring Di-gou back to family. Make him rid of Communist demon.

POPO. He will speak in tongue of fire. Like he does when he is a little boy with See-goh-poh. *(Wilbur enters the tennis court with an empty laundry basket. He heads for the barbecue. Joanne follows him.)*

JOANNE. *(To Wilbur.)* Hon, what are you going to do with those?

WILBUR. *(Referring to the burnt chicken.)* I'm just going to give them to Grizzly. *(He piles the chickens into the basket.)*

JOANNE. All right. *(She notices that the mess in the lanai has not been touched.)* Jenny! *(To Wilbur.)* But be careful not to give Grizzly any bones! *(Joanne exits.)*

WILBUR. *(To Ama and Popo.)* How you doin', Mom, Auntie?

AMA. *(To Popo, sotto voce.)* Kill and laugh.

WILBUR. Joanne tells me you're pretty excited about your brother's arrival—pretty understandable, after all these years—what's his name again? Di-ger, Di-gow, something...

AMA. Di-goo!

WILBUR. Yeah, right. Gotta remember that. Be pretty embarrassing if I said the wrong name. Di-gou.

POPO. Di-gou is not his name.

WILBUR. What? Not his—? What is it again? Di-gow? De—?

AMA. Di-gou?

WILBUR. Di-gou.

POPO. That is not his name.

WILBUR. Oh. It's the tones in Chinese, isn't it? I'm saying the wrong tone: Di-gou? Or Di-gou? Or—

POPO. Di-gou meaning is "second brother."

WILBUR. Oh, I see. It's not his name. Boy, do I feel ignorant in these situations. If only there were some way I could make sure I don't embarrass myself tonight.

AMA. Eat outside.

WILBUR. Outisde?

POPO. Or in kitchen.

WILBUR. In the kitchen? That's great! You two are real jokers, you know?

AMA. No. We are not.

WILBUR. C'mon. I should bring you down to the club someday. The guys never believe it when I tell them how much I love you two.

AMA. *(To Popo.)* Gao sai. *(Jenny enters the sunroom)*

WILBUR. Right. *"Gao sai"* to you, too. *(He starts to leave, sees Jenny.)* Wash your hands before you play with your grandmother.

JENNY. *(To Wilbur.)* Okay, Dad. *(To Ama.)* Do I have to, Ama?

AMA. No. Of course not.

JENNY. Can I ask you something personal?

AMA. Of course.

JENNY. Did Daddy just call you "dog shit"?

AMA. Jenny!

POPO. Yes. Very good!

JENNY. Doesn't that bother you?

POPO. *(To Ama.)* Her Chinese is improving!

JENNY. We learned it in Chinese school.

AMA. Jenny, you should not use this American word.

JENNY. Sorry. It just slipped out.

AMA. You do not use such word at school, no?

JENNY. Oh, no. Of course not.

AMA. You should not use anyplace.

JENNY. Right.

POPO. Otherwise—no good man wants marry you.

JENNY. You mean, no rich man.

AMA. No—money is not important.

POPO. As long as he is good man. *(Pause.)*

AMA. Christian.

POPO. Chinese.

AMA. Good education.

POPO. Good school.

AMA. Princeton.

POPO. Harvard.

AMA. Doctor.

POPO. Surgeon.

AMA. Brain surgeon.

POPO. Surgeon general.

AMA. Otherwise—you marry anyone that you like.

JENNY. Ama, Popo—look, I'm only seventeen.

POPO. True. But you can develop the good habits now.

JENNY. I don't want to get married till I'm at least thirty or something.

POPO. Thirty! By that time we are dead!

AMA. Gone to see God!

POPO. Lie in ground, arms cross!

JENNY. Look at it this way: how can I be a good mother if I have to follow my career around?

AMA. Your career will not require this.

JENNY. Yeah, it will. What if I have to go on tour?

AMA. Dental technicians do not tour.

AMA. Ama!

POPO. Only tour—one mouth to next mouth: "Hello. Clean your teeth?"

JENNY. Look, I'm telling you, I'm going to be a dancer.

AMA. We say—you can do both. Combine skills.

JENNY. That's ridiculous.

POPO. Be first dancing dental technician.

JENNY. I don't wanna be a dental technician!

POPO. Dancing dental technician very rare. You will be very popular.

JENNY. Why can't I be like Chester?

AMA. You cannot be like Chester.

JENNY. Why not!

POPO. You do not play violin. Chester does not dance. No hope.

JENNY. I know, but I mean, he's a musician. Why can't I be a dancer?

AMA. Chester—his work very dangerous.

JENNY. Dangerous?

AMA. He just receive new job—play with Boston Symphony.

JENNY. Yeah. I know. He's leaving tomorrow. So? What's so bad about Boston?

AMA. Conductor—Ozawa—he is Japanese.

JENNY. Oh, no. Not this again.

AMA. Very strict. If musicians miss one note, they must kill themself!

JENNY. Don't be ridiculous. That's no reason why I can't be like Chester.

POPO. But Chester—he makes plenty money.

JENNY. Yeah. Right. Now. But he has to leave home to do it, see? I want a carrer, too. So what if I never get married?

AMA. Jenny! You must remember—you come from family of See-goh-poh. She was a great evangelist.

JENNY. I know about See-goh-poh. She was your aunt.

AMA. First in family to become Christian.

POPO. She make this family chosen by God.

JENNY. To do what? Clean teeth?

AMA. Jenny!

JENNY. Look, See-goh-poh never got married because of her work, right?

AMA. See-goh-poh was marry to God.

POPO. When Di-gou arrive, he will tell you his testimony. How See-goh-poh change his life.

AMA. Before, he is like you. *(To Popo.)* You remember?

POPO. Yes. He is always so fussy.

JENNY. I'm not fussy.

AMA. Stubborn.

POPO. Complain this, complain that.

JENNY. I'm not complaining!

AMA. He will be very happy to meet you. Someone to complain with.

JENNY. I'm just telling you, there's no such thing as a dancing dental technician!

AMA. Good. You will be new discovery.

POPO. When Di-gou is a little boy, he never play with other children. He only read the books. Read books—and play tricks.

AMA. He is very naughty.

POPO. He tell other children there are ghosts hide inside the tree, behind the bush, in the bathroom at night.

AMA. One day, he feed snail poison to gardener.

POPO. Then, when he turns eight year old, See-goh-poh decide she will bring him on her evangelism tour. When he return, he has the tongue of fire.

JENNY. Oh, c'mon—those kind of things only happened in China.

AMA. No—they can happen here as well.

POPO. Di-gou at eight, he goes with See-goh-poh on her first evangelism tour—they travel all around Fukien—thirty day and night, preach to all villages. Five hundred people accept Christ on these thirty day and night, preach to all villages. Five hundred people accept Christ on these thirty day, and See-goh-poh heal many sick, restore ear to deaf, put tongue in mouth of dumb, all these thing and cast out the demon. Perhaps even one dead man—dead and wither—he rise up from his sleep. Di-gou see all this while carry See-goh-poh's bag and bring her food, ah? After thirty day, they return home. We have large banquet—perhaps twelve different dish that night—outside—underneath—ah—cloth. After we eat, See-goh-poh- say, "Now is time for Family Devotions, and this time, he will lead." See-goh-poh point to Di-gou, who is still a boy, but he walk up in front of table and begin to talk and flame begin to come from his mouth, over his head. Fire. Fire, all around. His voice—so loud—praise and testify the miracle of God. Louder and louder, more and more fire, till entire sky fill with light, does not seem to be night, like middle of day, like twelve noon. When we finish talk, sun has already rise, and cloth over our head, it is all burn, gone, ashes blow away. *(Joanne enters, pulling Chester behind. He carries a suitcase.)*

JOANNE. Look who's here!

POPO. Chester—good you decide to come.

JOANNE. He looked lost. This house isn't that big, you know. *(Exits.)*

AMA. *(To Chester.)* You come for reunion with Di-gou. Very good.

CHESTER. Uh—look, I really can't stay. I have to finish packing.

AMA. You must stay—see Di-gou!

CHESTER. But I'm leaving tomorrow. *(Doorbell.)*

CHESTER. Oh no.

JOANNE. Can someone get that? ⎫

JENNY. Too late! ⎬ *(Simultaneously.)*

POPO. Di-gou! ⎭

AMA. *(To Chester.)* You must! This will be Di-gou! *(Wilbur crosses with basket, now full of chicken bones.)*

WILBUR. I'll get it. Chester, good to see you made it. *(Exits.)*

JENNY. He almost didn't.

CHESTER. I'm really short on time. I gotta go. I'll see you tomorrow at the airport.

POPO. Chester! When Di-gou arrive, he must see whole family! You stay! *(Chester pauses, decides to stay.)*

CHESTER. *(To Jenny.)* This is ridiculous. I can't stay.

JENNY. I always have to. Just grin a lot when you meet this guy. Then everyone will be happy.

CHESTER. I don't wanna meet this guy! *(Wilbur enters with Hannah and Robert, who are Chester's parents. Hannah is Popo's daughter. They are five to ten years older than Joanne and Wilbur.)*

WILBUR. *(To Robert.)* What? What do you mean?

AMA. *(Stands up on a chair; a speech.)* Di-gou, thirty year have pass since we last see you—

WILBUR. *(To Ama.)* Not now, Ma.

AMA. Do you still love God?

ROBERT. What do you mean, "What do you mean?" That's what I mean.

HANNAH. He wasn't there, Wilbur. *(To Ama.)* Auntie! Di-gou isn't with us.

AMA. What? How can this be?

ROBERT. Those Chinese airliners—all junk stuffs—so inefficent.

AMA. Where is he?

POPO. *(To Robert.)* You sure you look close?

ROBERT. What "look close"? We just waited for everyone to get off the plane.

AMA. Where is he?

HANNAH. *(To Ama.)* We don't know, Auntie! *(To Chester.)* Chester, are you packed?

AMA. Don't know?

CHESTER. *(To Hannah.)* No, I'm not. And I'm really in a hurry.

HANNAH. You're leaving tomorrow! Why aren't you packed?

CHESTER. I'm trying to, Mom. *(Robert pulls out a newspaper clipping, shows it to Chester.)*

ROBERT. Look, son, I called the Chinese paper, used a little of my influences—they did a story on you—here.

CHESTER. *(Looks at clipping.)* I can't read this, Dad! It's in Chinese!

ROBERT. *(Takes back clipping.)* Little joke , there.

AMA. *(To anyone who will listen.)* Where is he?

HANNAH. *(To Ama.)* Auntie, ask Wilbur. *(To Chester.)* Get packed!

CHESTER. All right!

WILBUR. *(Trying to explain to Ama.)* Well, Mom, they said he wasn't at—

AMA. *(Ignoring Wilbur totally.)* Where is he?! *(Robert continues to study the newspaper clipping, points a section out to Chester.)*

ROBERT. Here—this is where it talks about my bank.

CHESTER. I'm going to pack.

HANNAH. *(To Chester.)* Going?

CHESTER. *(To Hannah.)* You said I should—

HANNAH. *(To Chester.)* You have to stay and see Di-gou! *(Wilbur makes another attempt to explain the situation to Ama.)*

WILBUR. *(To Ama.)* See, Mom, I guess—

AMA. *(Ignoring him again.)* Where is he? *(Robert continues studying his clipping. Oblivious.)*

ROBERT. *(Translating, to Chester.)* It says, "Great Chinese violinist will conduct and solo with New York Philharmonic."

CHESTER. What? It says what?

HANNAH. *(To Chester.)* You came without being packed? *(Ama decides to look for Di-gou on her own, and starts searching the house.)*

AMA. Di-gou! Di-gou!

WILBUR. *(Following Ama.)* Ma, listen. I'll explain.

HANNAH. *(To Chester.)* How can you be so inefficient?

CHESTER. *(To Robert.)* Dad, I just got a job playing in the violin section in Boston.

AMA. Di-gou! Di-gou!

CHESTER. *(To Robert.)* I'm not conducting, and—

ROBERT. *(To Chester.)* Ssssh! I know. But good publicity—for the bank.

HANNAH. *(To Chester.)* Well, I'll help you pack later. But you have to stay till Di-gou arrives. Aheesh!

CHESTER. I can't believe this!

AMA. *(Continuing her search.)* Di-gou! Are you already in bathroom? *(Exits.)*

HANNAH. *(To Ama.)* Auntie, he wasn't at the airport! *(To Wilbur.)* Why didn't you tell her?

WILBUR. *(Following Ama.)* I'm trying! I'm trying! *(Exits.)*

ROBERT. It's those Communist airlines, I'm telling you. Inefficient.

HANNAH. We asked at the desk. They didn't have a flight list.

AMA. *(Entering.)* Then where is he?

WILBUR. *(Entering, in despair.)* Joanne, will you come here?

ROBERT. They probably left him in Guam.

POPO. *(To Robert.)* We give you that photograph. You remember to bring it?

ROBERT. Of course I remembered.

HANNAH. *(To Popo.)* Mom, it's not Robert's fault.

POPO. *(To Hannah.)* Should leave him. *(Refers to Robert in car.)*

HANNAH. I tried.

ROBERT. In the car?

HANNAH. He wanted to come in.

ROBERT. It's hot in the car!

AMA. *(To Robert.)* Suffer, good for you.

POPO. *(To Hannah.)* You cannot control your husband.

ROBERT. I suffer enough.

HANNAH. He said he could help.

POPO. He is wrong again.

AMA. What to do now? *(Jenny exits in the confusion; Joanne enters.)*

JOANNE. What's wrong now?

WILBUR. They lost your uncle.

JOANNE. Who lost him?

HANNAH. We didn't lose him.

62

AMA. *(To Robert.)* You ask at airport desk?

ROBERT. I'm telling you, he's in Guam.

JOANNE. *(To Hannah.)* How could you lose a whole uncle?

HANNAH. We never had him to begin with!

JOANNE. So where is he?

ROBERT. Guam, I'm telling—!

POPO. *(To Robert.)* Guam, Guam! Shut mouth or go there yourself!

HANNAH. *(A general announcement.)* We don't know where he is!

JOANNE. Should I call the police?

WILBUR. You might have looked longer at the airport.

HANNAH. That's what I said, but he *(Refers to Robert.)* said, "Aaah, too much trouble!"

POPO. *(To Robert.)* See? You do not care about people from other province besides Shanghai.

ROBERT. *(To Popo.)* Mom, I care. It's just that—

POPO. *(To Robert.)* Your father trade with Japanese during war.

WILBUR. Huh?

ROBERT. Mom, let's not start that—

POPO. Not like our family. We die first!

WILBUR. What's all this about?

ROBERT. Hey, let's not bring up all this other junk, right?

POPO. *(To Robert.)* You are ashamed.

ROBERT. The airport is a big place.

WILBUR. *(To Robert.)* Still, you should've been able to spot an old Chinese man.

ROBERT. Everyone on that plane was an old Chinese man!

AMA. True. All Communist look alike.

HANNAH. Hold it, everybody! *(Pause.)* Listen, Di-gou has this address, right?

AMA. No.

HANNAH. No? *(To Popo.)* Mom, you said he did.

POPO. Yes. He does.

AMA. *(To Popo.)* Yes? But I did not write to him.

POPO. I did.

AMA. Now, Communist—they will know this address.

POPO. Never mind.

AMA. No safety. Bomb us.

HANNAH. Okay, he has this address, and he can speak English—after all, he went to medical school here, right? So he shouldn't have any problem.

JOANNE. What an introduction to America.

HANNAH. All we can do is wait.

ROBERT. We went up to all these old Chinese men at the airport, asked them, "Are you our Di-gou?" They all said yes. What could we do? They all looked drunk, bums.

JOANNE. Maybe they're all still wandering through the metal detectors, looking for their families, and will continue till they die. *(Chester, wanders onto the tennis court, observes the following section from far U.)* I must have been only about seven the last time Di-gou visited us in the Philippines.

AMA. Less.

JOANNE. Maybe less.

WILBUR. Honey, I'm sure everyone here has a memory, too. You don't see them babbling about it, do you?

JOANNE. The last thing I remember about Di-gou, he was trying to convince you grown-ups to leave the Philippines and return to China. There was a terrible fight—one of the worst that ever took place in our complex. I guess he wanted you to join the Revolution. The fight was so loud that all our servants gathered around the windows to watch.

AMA. They did this?

POPO. Shoot them.

JOANNE. I guess this was just around 1949. Finally, Di-gou left, calling you all sorts of terrible names. On his way out, he set fire to one of our warehouses. All us kids sat around while the servants tried to put it out.

POPO. No. That was not a warehouse.

HANNAH. Yeah, Joanne—the warehouses were concrete, remember?

JOANNE. *(To Hannah.)* But don't you remember a fire?

HANNAH. Yes.

POPO. I think he burn a pile of trash.

ROBERT. *(To Wilbur.)* I know how you feel. They're always yap-yap-yapping about their family stories—you'd think they were the only family in China. *(To Hannah.)* I have memories, tóo.

HANNAH. You don't remember anything. You have a terrible memory.

ROBERT. Look, when I was kidnapped, I didn't know—

HANNAH. Sssssh!

JOANNE. Quiet, Robert!

POPO. Like broken record—ghang, ghang, ghang.

WILBUR. *(To Robert.)* I tell you what: you wanna take a look at my collection of tax shelters?

ROBERT. Same old stuff?

WILBUR. No. Some new ones. *(They exit. Di-gou appears on the tennis court; only Chester sees him, but Chester says nothing. Chester watches Di-gou watching the women.)*

JOANNE. Anyway, he set fire to something and the flames burned long into the night. One servant was even killed in it, if I remember correctly. I think Matthew's nursemaid was trying to put it out when her dress caught fire and, like a fool, she ran screaming all over the complex. All the adults were too busy to hear her, I guess, and all the kids just sat there and watched this second fire, moving in circles and screaming. By morning, both fires were out, and our tutors came as usual. But that day, nothing functioned just right—I think the water pipes broke in Sah-Zip's room, the cars wouldn't start—something—all I remember is servants running around all day with one tool or another. And that was how Di-gou left Manila for the last time. Left Manila and returned to China—in two fires—one which moved—and a great rush of handymen. *(Di-gou is now sitting in their midst in the sunroom. He puts down his suitcase. They turn and see him. He sticks his thumb out, as if for hitchhiking, but it is pointed in the wrong direction.)*

DI-GOU. "Going my way?"

AMA. Di-gou!

DI-GOU. "Hey, baby, got a lift?"

POPO. You see? Our family members will always return.

JOANNE. *(To Di-gou.)* Are you—? Oh, you're—? Well, nice— How did you get here?

DI-GOU. *(Pulls a book out of his jacket.)* Our diplomacy handbook. Very useful.

POPO. Welcome to America!

DI-GOU. *(Referring to the handbook.)* It says, "When transportation is needed, put your thumb as if to plug a hole."

AMA. *(On chair.)* Di-gou, thirty year have passed—

DI-GOU. *(Still reading.)* "And say, 'Going my way?'"

AMA. Do you still believe in God?

DI-GOU. "Or, 'Hey, baby, got a lift?'"

AMA. Do you?

HANNAH. *(To Ama.)* Auntie, he's explaining something.

DI-GOU. It worked! I am here!

AMA. *(Getting down off chair.)* Still as stubborn as before.

DI-GOU. Hello, my sisters.

POPO. Hello, Di-gou. This is my daughter, Hannah.

HANNAH. *(To Di-gou.)* Were you at the airport? We were waiting for you.

DI-GOU. Hannah. Oh, last time, you were just a baby.

AMA. *(Introducing Joanne.)* And Joanne, remember?

JOANNE. Hello, Di-gou. How was your flight?

DI-GOU. Wonderful, wonderful.

POPO. Where is Chester? Chester! *(Chester enters the lanai.)* Him—this is number one grandson.

DI-GOU. Oh, you are Chester. You are the violinist, yes?

CHESTER. You're Di-gou?

DI-GOU. Your parents are so proud of you.

HANNAH. We are not. He's just a kid who needs to pack.

AMA. Where is Jenny? Jenny!

HANNAH. *(To Di-gou.)* We figured you'd be able to get here by yourself.

DI-GOU. Oh, yes. *(He sticks out his thumb. Jenny enters.)*

JOANNE. Jenny! Say, "Hi, Di-gou."

66

JENNY. Hi, Di-gou.

DI-GOU. *(To Joanne.)* This is your daughter?

JOANNE. Yes. Jenny. *(Pause.)* Jenny, say, "Hi, Di-gou."

JENNY. Mom, I just did!.

JOANNE. Oh. Right.

JENNY. Will you cool out?

DI-GOU. Jenny, the last time I saw your mother, she was younger than you are now.

JENNY. He's kinda cute.

JOANNE. Jenny, your granduncle is not cute.

DI-GOU. Thank you.

JENNY. *(To Joanne.)* Can I go now?

AMA. Why you always want to go?

JENNY. Sorry, Ama. Busy.

JOANNE. *(Allowing Jenny to leave.)* All right.

DI-GOU. *(To Jenny.)* What are you doing?

JENNY. Huh? Reading.

DI-GOU. Oh. Schoolwork.

JENNY. Nah. *Vogue. (Exits.)*

JOANNE. I've got to see about dinner. *(To Hannah.)* Can you give me a hand? I want to use my new Cuisinart.

HANNAH. All right. What do you want to make?

JOANNE. I don't know. What does a Cuisinart do? *(Hannah and Joanne exit; Di-gou, Ama, Popo, and Chester are left in the sunroom.)*

AMA. Di-gou, thirty year have pass. Do you still love God?

DI-GOU. Thirty-three.

AMA. Ah?

POPO. 1949 to 1982. Thirty-three. He is correct.

AMA. Oh. But you do still love God? Like before?

DI-GOU. You know, sisters, after you left China, I learned that I never did believe in God. *(Pause.)*

AMA. What!

POPO. How can you say this?

CHESTER. Ama, Popo, don't start in on that—he just got here.

POPO. You defend him?

AMA. *(Chasing Chester out to tennis court.)* You both are influence by bad people.

POPO. Spend time with bums! Communist bum, musician bum, both same.

DI-GOU. Just to hear my sisters after all these years—you may speak whatever you like.

AMA. Do you still love God?

DI-GOU. I have much love.

AMA. For God?

DI-GOU. For my sisters. *(Pause.)*

POPO. You are being very difficult.

AMA. You remember when you first become Christian?

POPO. You travel with See-goh-poh on her first evangelism tour? Before we move to Philippines and you stay in China? Remember? You speak in tongues of fire.

DI-GOU. I was only eight years old. That evening is a blur to me.

AMA. Tonight—we have family devotions. You can speak again. Miracles. You still believe in miracles?

DI-GOU. It is a miracle that I am here again with you!

POPO. Why you always change subject? You remember Ah Hong? Your servant? How See-goh-poh cast out his opium demon?

DI-GOU. I don't think that happened.

AMA. Yes! Remember? After evangelism tour—she cast out his demon.

POPO. Ah Hong tell stories how he eats opium, then he can see everything so clear, like— uh—glass. He can see even through wall, he say, and can see—ah—all the way through floor. Yes! He say he can see through ground, all the way to hell. And he talk with Satan and demon who pretend to be Ah Hong's dead uncles. You should remember.

DI-GOU. I vaguely recall some such stories. *(Di-gou opens up his suitcase during Popo's following speech and takes out two small Chinese toys and a small Chinese flag. He shows them to Popo, but she tries to ignore them.)*

POPO. Demon pretend to be ghost, then show himself everyplace to Ah Hong—in kitchen, in well, in barn, in street of village. Always just sit there, never talk, never move, just sit. So See-goh-poh come, call on God, say only, "Demon begone."

AMA. And from then on, no more ghost, no more opium.

POPO. You—you so happy, then. You say, you will also cast out the demon.

DI-GOU. We were all just children. *(He lines the toys up on the floor.)*

AMA. But you have faith of a child.

DI-GOU. Ah Hong didn't stop eating opium, though. He just needed money. That's why two years later, he was fired.

AMA. Ah Hong never fired!

POPO. I do not think so.

DI-GOU. Yes, my tenth, eleventh birthday, he was fired.

AMA. No—remember? Ah Hong die many year later—just before you come to America for college.

DI-GOU. No, he was fired before then.

POPO. No. Before you leave, go to college, you must prepare your own suitcase. *(To Ama.)* Bad memory.

AMA. Brainwash. *(Robert and Wilbur enter; Chester exits off the tennis court. Robert and Wilbur surround Di-gou.)*

ROBERT and WILBUR. Welcome!

WILBUR. How you doing, Di-gow?

ROBERT. *(Correcting Wilbur.)* Di-gou!

WILBUR. Oh, right. "Di-gou."

ROBERT. *(To Di-gou.)* We tried to find you at the airport.

WILBUR. *(To Di-gou.)* That means "second brother."

ROBERT. So, you escaped the Communists, huh?

WILBUR. Robert and I were just—

ROBERT. Little joke, there.

WILBUR. —looking at my collection of tax shelters.

ROBERT. China's pretty different now, huh?

WILBUR. You care to take a look?

ROBERT. I guess there's never a dull moment—

WILBUR. Probably no tax shelters, either.

ROBERT. —waiting for the next cultural revoluation.

WILBUR. Oh, Robert!

ROBERT. Little joke, there.

WILBUR. *(To Di-gou.)* That's how he *(Refers to Robert.)* does business.

ROBERT. Of course, I respect China.

WILBUR. He says these totally outrageous things.

ROBERT. But your airlines—so inefficient.

WILBUR. And people remember him.

ROBERT. How long were you in Guam?

WILBUR. *(To Robert.)* He wasn't in Guam!

ROBERT. No?

WILBUR. *(To Di-gou.)* Well, we're going to finish up the tour.

ROBERT. My shelters are all at my house.

WILBUR. Feel welcome to come along.

ROBERT. His *(Refers to Wilbur.)* are kid stuff. Who wants land in Montana?

WILBUR. *(To Robert.)* Hey—I told you. I need the loss. *(Wilbur and Robert exit, leaving Di-gou with Ama and Popo. There is a long silence.)*

DI-GOU. Who are they?

POPO. Servants.

AMA. Don't worry. They will eat outside. In America, servants do not take over their masters' house.

DI-GOU. What are you talking about?

AMA. We know. In China now, servants beat their masters.

DI-GOU. Don't be ridiculous. I have a servant. A chauffeur. *(Robert reenters.)*

ROBERT. Hey, Di-gou—we didn't even introduce ourselves.

DI-GOU. Oh, my sisters explained it to me.

ROBERT. I'm Robert. Hannah's my wife. *(Robert puts his arm around Di-gou.)* When we married, I had nothing. I was working in grocery stores, fired from one job after another. But she could tell— I had a good heart.

DI-GOU. It is good to see servants marrying into the moneyed

70

ranks. We are not aware of such progress by even the lowest classes.
(Pause.)

ROBERT. Huh?

DI-GOU. To come to this—from the absolute bottom of society.

ROBERT. Wait, wait. I mean, sure, I made progress, but "the bottom of society"? That's stretching it some, wouldn't you say?

DI-GOU. Did you meet Hannah while preparing her food?

ROBERT. Huh? No, we met at a foreign students' dance at UCLA.

DI-GOU. Oh. You attended university?

ROBERT. Look, I'm not a country kid. It's not like I was that poor. I'm from Shanghai, you know.

POPO. *(To Robert.)* Ssssh! Neighbors will hear!

ROBERT. I'm cosmopolitan. So when I went to college, I just played around at first. That's the beauty of the free-enterprise system, Di-gou. If you wanna be a bum, it lets you be a bum. I wasted my time, went out with all those American girls.

POPO. One girl.

ROBERT. Well, one was more serious, a long commitment...

POPO. Minor.

DI-GOU. What?

POPO. He go out with girl—only fifteen year old.

ROBERT. I didn't know!

POPO. *(To Robert.)* How come you cannot ask?

ROBERT. I was just an FOB. This American girl—she talked to me—asked me out—kissed me on first date—and I thought, "Land of opportunity!" Anyway, I decided to turn my back on China.

POPO. *(To Di-gou.)* He cannot even ask girl how old.

ROBERT. This is my home. When I wanted to stop being a bum, make money, it let me. That's America!

DI-GOU. I also attended university. Columbia Medical School.

ROBERT. Right. My wife told me.

71

POPO. *(To Robert.)* But he does not date the minor!

ROBERT. *(To Popo.)* How was I supposed to know? She looked fully developed! *(Ama and Popo leave in disgust, leaving Robert alone with Di-gou. To Di-gou.)* Well, then, you must understand American ways.

DI-GOU. It has been some time since I was in America.

ROBERT. Well, it's improved a lot, lemme tell you. Look, I have a friend who's an immigration lawyer. If you want to stay here, he can arrange it.

DI-GOU. Oh, no. The thought never even—

ROBERT. I know, but listen. I did it. Never had any regrets. We might be able to get your family over, too.

DI-GOU. Robert, I cannot leave China.

ROBERT. Huh? Look, Di-gou, people risk their lives to come to America. If only you could talk to—to the boat people.

DI-GOU. Uh—the food here looks very nice.

ROBERT. Huh? Oh, help yourself, Go ahead.

DI-GOU. Thank you. I will wait.

ROBERT. No, go on!

DI-GOU. Thank you, but—

ROBERT. Look, in America, there's so much, we don't have to be polite at all!

DI-GOU. Please—I'm not yet hungry.

ROBERT. Us Chinese, we love to eat, right? Well, here in America, we can be pigs!

DI-GOU. I'm not hungry.

ROBERT. I don't see why you can't—? Look. *(He picks up a piece of food, a bao.)* See? *(He stuffs the whole thing into his mouth.)* Pigs!

DI-GOU. Do you mind? I told you, I'm not—

ROBERT. I know. You're not hungry. Think I'm hungry? No, sir! What do I have to do to convince you? Here. *(He drops a tray of guo-tieh on the ground, begins stomping them.)* This is the land of plenty!

DI-GOU. Ai! Robert! *(Robert continues stomping them like roaches.)*

ROBERT. There's one next to your foot! *(He stomps it.)* Gotcha!

DI-GOU. Please! It is not right to step on food!

ROBERT. "Right?" Now, see, that's your problem in the P.R.C.—lots of justice, but you don't produce. *(Wilbur enters, catching Robert in the act.)*

WILBUR. Robert? What are you—? What's all this?

ROBERT. *(Stops stomping.)* What's the big deal? You got a cleaning woman, don't you? *(Jenny enters.)*

JENNY. Time to eat yet? *(She sees the mess.)* Blaagh. *(Hannah enters.)*

HANNAH. What's all this?

JENNY. Never mind. *(Jenny exits; Wilbur points to Robert, indicating to Hannah that Robert is responsible for the mess. Ama and Popo also enter at this moment, and see Wilbur's indication.)*

DI-GOU. In China, the psychological problems of wealth are a great concern.

POPO. Ai! Who can clean up after man like this!

WILBUR. Robert, I just don't think this is proper.

AMA. Wilbur—not clean himself.

ROBERT. Quiet! You all make a big deal out of nothing!

DI-GOU. I am a doctor. I understand.

POPO. But Robert—he also has the fungus feet.

ROBERT. Shut up, everybody! Will you all just shut up? I was showing Di-gou American ways! *(Wilbur takes Di-gou's arm.)*

WILBUR. *(To Di-gou.)* Uh—come out here. I'll show you some American ways. *(Wilbur and Di-gou go out to the tennis court.)*

ROBERT. *(To Wilbur.)* What do you know about American ways? You were born here!

POPO. *(To Ama.)* Exercise—good for him.

ROBERT. Only us immmigrants really know American ways!

POPO. *(To Ama, pinching her belly.)* Good for here.

HANNAH. *(To Robert.)* Shut up, dear. You've done enough damage today. *(Wilbur gets Di-gou a racket.)*

AMA. *(To Popo.)* In China, he *(Refers to Di-gou.)* receives plenty exercise. Whenever Communists, they come torture him.

73

WILBUR. *(On the tennis court, to Di-gou.)* I'll set up the machine. *(He goes off.)*

ROBERT. *(In sunroom, looking at tennis court.)* What's so American about tennis?

HANNAH. *(To Robert.)* Yes, dear.

ROBERT. You all ruined it!

HANNAH. You ruined the *guo-tieh* in defense of America?

DI-GOU. *(To Wilbur.)* I have not played tennis since my college days at Columbia.

ROBERT. *(To Hannah.)* He *(Refers to Di-gou.)* was being so cheap! Like this was a poor country!

HANNAH. He's lived in America before, dear.

ROBERT. That was years ago. When we couldn't even buy a house in a place like this.

HANNAH. We still can't.

ROBERT. What?

HANNAH. Let's face it. We still can't afford—

ROBERT. That's not what I mean, stupid! I mean, when we wouldn't be able to because we're Chinese! He doesn't know the new America. I was making a point and you all ruined it!

HANNAH. Yes, dear. Now let's go in and watch the Betamax.

ROBERT. No!

HANNAH. C'mon! *(Robert and Hannah exit. On the tennis court, Di-gou and Wilbur stand next to each other, facing offstage. A machine offstage begins to shoot tennis balls at them, each ball accompanied by a small explosive sound. A ball goes by; Di-gou tries to hit it, but it is too high for him. Two more balls go by, but they are also out of Di-gou's reach. A fourth ball is shot out, which hits Wilbur.)*

WILBUR. Aaaah! *(Balls are being shot out much faster now, pummeling Wilbur and Di-gou. Ama and Popo continue to sit in the sunroom, staring away from the tennis court, peaceful and oblivious.)*

DI-GOU. Aaah!

WILBUR. I don't—! This never happened—!

DI-GOU. Watch out!

WILBUR. I'll turn off the machine.

DI-GOU. Good luck! Persevere! Overcome! Oh! Watch—! *(A*

74

volley of balls drives Wilbur back. Ama and Popo hear the commotion, look over to the tennis court. The balls stop shooting out.)

ROBERT. Tennis.

AMA. A fancy machine. *(They return to looking downstage. The balls begin again.)*

WILBUR. Oh, no!

AMA. Wilbur—he is such a bad loser.

POPO. Good exercise, huh? His age—good for here. *(She pinches her belly.)*

DI-GOU. I will perserve! *(Di-gou tries to get to the machine, is driven back.)*

WILBUR. No! Di-gow!

DI-GOU. I am overcome!

WILBUR. Joanne! *(He begins crawling like a guerrilla toward the machine and finally makes it offstage. The balls stop, presumably because Wilbur reached the machine. Di-gou runs off the court.)*

DI-GOU. *(Breathless.)* Is it time yet...that we may cease to have...such enjoyment? *(Wilbur crosses back onto the tennis court and into the lanai.)*

WILBUR. *(To offstage.)* Joanne! This machine's too fast. I don't pay good money to be attacked by my possessions! *(Exits. Ama and Popo get up, exit into the house, applauding Di-gou as they go, for his exercise.)*

AMA and POPO. *(Clapping.)* Good, good, very good! *(Di-gou is left alone on the tennis court. He is hit by a lone tennis ball. Chester enters, with a violin case. It is obvious that he has thrown that ball.)*

CHESTER. Quite a workout, there.

DI-GOU. America is full of surprises—why do all these products function so poorly?

CHESTER. Looks like "Made in U.S." is gonna become synonymous with defective workmanship. *(Pause.)* You wanna see my violin?

DI-GOU. I would love to.

CHESTER. I thought you might. Here. *(He removes the violin from its case.)*

CHESTER. See? No "Made in U.S." label.

DI-GOU. It's beautiful.

CHESTER. Careful! The back has a lacquer which never dries—so don't touch it, or you'll leave your fingerprints in it forever.

DI-GOU. Imagine that. After I die, someone could be playing a violin with my fingerprint.

CHESTER. Funny, isn't it?

DI-GOU. You know, I used to play violin.

CHESTER. Really?

DI-GOU. Though I never had as fine an instrument as this.

CHESTER. Try it. Go ahead.

DI-GOU. No. Please. I get more pleasure looking at it than I would playing it. But I would get the most pleasure hearing you play.

CHESTER. No.

DI-GOU. Please?

CHESTER. All right. Later. How long did you play?

DI-GOU. Some years. During the Cultural Revolution, I put it down.

CHESTER. Must've been tough, huh? *(Chester directs Di-gou's attention to the back of his violin.)* Look—the back's my favorite part.

DI-GOU. China is my home, my work. I had to stay there. *(Di-gou looks at the back of the violin.)* Oh—the way the light reflects—look. And I can see myself in it.

CHESTER. Yeah. Nice, huh?

DI-GOU. So you will take this violin and make music around the world.

CHESTER. Around the world? Oh, you probably got a misleading press clipping. See, my dad...

DI-GOU. Very funny.

CHESTER. *(Smiling.)* Yeah. See, I'm just playing in the Boston Symphony. I'm leaving tomorrow.

DI-GOU. I am fortunate, then, to come today, or perhaps I would never meet you.

CHESTER. You know, I wasn't even planning to come here.

DI-GOU. That would be terrible. You know, in China, my wife and I had no children—for the good of the state. *(Di-gou moves to where he left the Chinese toys earlier in the act. He picks them up and studies them.)* All these years, I try to imagine—what does Hannah look like? What does her baby look like? Now, I finally visit and what do I find? A young man. A violinist. The baby has long since disappeared. And I learn I'll never know the answer to my question. *(Silence.)*

CHESTER. Di-gou, why did you come here?

DI-GOU. My wife has died, I'm old. I've come for my sisters.

CHESTER. Well, I hope you're not disappinted to come here and see your sisters, your family, carry on like this.

DI-GOU. They are still my sisters.

CHESTER. I'm leaving here. Like you did.

DI-GOU. But, Chester, I've found that I cannot leave the family. Today—look!—I follow them across an ocean.

CHESTER. You know, they're gonna start bringing you to church.

DI-GOU. No. My sisters and their religion are two different things.

CHESTER. No, they're not. You've been away. You've forgotten. This family breathes for God. Ever since your aunt, See-goh-poh.

DI-GOU. See-goh-poh is not the first member of this family.

CHESTER. She's the first Christian.

DI-GOU. There are faces back further than you can see. Faces long before the white missionaries arrived in China. Here. *(He holds Chester's violin so that its back is facing Chester, and uses it like a mirror.)* Look here. At your face. Study your face and you will see—the shape of your face is the shape of faces back many generations—across an ocean, in another soil. You must become one with your family before you can hope to live away from it.

CHESTER. Oh, sure, there're faces. But they don't matter here. See-goh-poh's face is the only one that has any meaning here.

DI-GOU. No. The stories written on your face are the ones you must believe.

CHESTER. Stories? I see stories, Di-gou. All around me. This house tells a story. The days of the week tell a story.—Sunday is service, Wednesday and Friday are fellowship, Thursday is visitation. Even the furniture tells stories. Look around. See-goh-poh is sitting in every chair. There's nothing for me here.

DI-GOU. I am here.

CHESTER. You? All right. Here. *(Chester turns the back of the violin toward Di-gou, again using it like a mirror.)* You look. You wanna know what I see? I see the shape of your face changing. And with it, a mind, a will, as different as the face. If you stay with them, your old self will go, and in its place will come a new man, an old man, a man who'll pray.

DI-GOU. Chester, you are in America. If you deny those who share your blood, what do you have in this country?

AMA. *(From offstage.)* All right? Ready?

CHESTER. Your face is changing, Di-gou. Before you know it, you'll be praying and speaking in tongues.

AMA. *(Still offstage.)* One, two, three, four! *(The "Hallelujah Chorus" begins. The choir enters, consisting of Wilbur, Joanne, Robert, Hannah, and Popo. They are led by Ama, who stands at a movable podium which is being pushed into the room by Robert and Wilbur as they sing. The choir heads for the center of the room, where the podium comes to rest, with Ama still on it, and the "Hallelujah Chorus" ends. Robert begins singing the tenor aria "Every Valley Shall Be Exalted." from Handel's Messiah.)*

ROBERT. "Every valley, every valley..."

HANNAH. Quiet, Robert!

ROBERT. But I want my solo!

JOANNE. *(To Robert.)* Ssssh! We already decided this.

ROBERT. *(Continuing to sing.)* "...shall be exalted..."

JOANNE. *(Yelling offstage.)* Jenny!

AMA. *(To Robert.)* Time for Family Devotions! Set up room! *(They begin to arrange the room like a congregation hall, with the pulpit up front.)*

ROBERT. But it's a chance to hear my beautiful voice.

JENNY. *(From offstage.)* Yeah! What?

POPO. *(To Robert.)* Hear at home, hear in car. Now set up room.

JOANNE. *(Yelling offstage.)* Jenny! Devotions!

JENNY. *(From offstage.)* Aw, Mom.

JOANNE. *(Yelling offstage.)* Devotions!

JENNY. *(Entering.)* All right.

ROBERT. *(To Hannah.)* You know what this is? This is the breakdown of family authority.

HANNAH. *(To Robert.)* You have all the authority, dear. Now shut up. *(Jenny goes over to Chester.)*

JENNY. Hey, you still here? I thought for sure you'd have split by now.

CHESTER. I will.

JENNY. You gotta take it easier. Do like me. I act all lotus blossom for them. I say, "Hi, uncle this and auntie that." It's easy.

ROBERT. Look—all this free time. *(Sings.)* "Every valley..."

POPO. Shoot him! *(The room is set up.)*

AMA. We begin! Family Devotions! *(Ama flips a switch. A neon cross is lit up.)*

JENNY. *(To Chester.)* Looks like a disco. *(Everyone is seated except Di-gou. The rest of the family waits for him. He walks over and sits down. Ama bows down to pray. Everyone bows except Chester and Di-gou, but since all other eyes are closed, no one notices their noncompliance. Ama begins to pray.)*

AMA. Dear Father, when we think of your great mercy to this family, we can only feel so grateful, privilege to be family chose for your work. You claim us to be yours, put your mark on our heart. *(Chester gets up, picks up his violin, gets Di-gou's attention.)* Your blessing begin many year ago in China. *(Chester begins playing; his music serves as underscoring to Ama's prayer.)* When See-goh-poh, she hear your word—from missionary. Your spirit, it touch her heart, she accept you, she speak in tongue of fire. *(Chester begins to move out of the room as he plays.)* You continue, bless See-goh-poh. She become agent of God, bring light to whole family, until we are convert, we become shining light for you all through Amoy. *(Chester stops playing, looks at Di-gou, waves good-bye, and exits. Di-gou gets up, walks to where Chester was standing before he left, and waves good-bye.)* Let us praise your victory over Satan. Praise your power over demon.

Praise miracle over our own sinful will. Praise your victory over even our very hearts. Amen. *(Ama conducts the choir in the ending of the "Hallelujah Chorus." As they sing, she notices Di-gou's chair is empty. She turns and sees him waving. They look at each other as the "Hallelujah Chorus" continues. Curtain.)*

END OF ACT ONE

ACT II

*A moment later. As the curtain rises, all are in the same
positions they occupied at the end of Act I. Ama and Di-gou are
looking at each other. The choir ends the "Hallelujah Chorus."
Di-gou walks back toward his chair, and sits. Ama notices that
Chester's seat is empty.*

AMA. Where is Chester?

HANNAH. I heard his violin.

AMA. This is family devotions.

ROBERT. The kid's got a mind of his own.

HANNAH. He probably went home to pack, Auntie. He's really
in a hurry.

JENNY. Can I go look?

AMA. Why everyone want to go?

JENNY. But he forgot his suitcase. *(She points to the green suitcase,
which Chester has left behind.)*

POPO. *(To Jenny.)* Di-gou, he will want to hear you give testimony. *(Jenny sits back down.)*

AMA. Now—Special Testimony. Let us tell of God's blessing!
Who will have privilege? Special Testimony! Who will be first to
praise? *(Silence.)* He is in our presence! Open His arms to us!
(Silence.) He is not going to wait forever—you know this! He is
very busy! *(Robert stands up, starts to head for podium. Popo notices
that Robert has risen, points to him.)*

POPO. No! Not him!

AMA. *(To Robert.)* He is very bored with certain people who say
same thing over and over again.

WILBUR. Why don't we sit down, Robert?

JENNY. C'mon, Uncle Robert.

HANNAH. Dear, forget it, all right?

ROBERT. But she needed someone to start. I just—

POPO. *(To Robert.)* She did not include you.

WILBUR. Can't you see how bored they are with that, Robert?

ROBERT. Bored.

WILBUR. Everybody else has forgotten it.

ROBERT. Forgotten it? They can't.

JOANNE. We could if you'd stop talking about it.

ROBERT. But there's something new!

WILBUR. Of course. There always is.

ROBERT. There is!

JOANNE. *(To Wilbur.)* Don't pay attention, dear. It just encourages him.

WILBUR. *(To Joanne.)* Honey, are you trying to advise *me* on how to be diplomatic?

JOANNE. I'm only saying, if you let Hannah—

WILBUR. You're a real stitch, you know that? You really are.

JOANNE. Hannah's good at keeping him quiet.

ROBERT. Quiet?

WILBUR. *(To Joanne.)* Look, who was voted "Mr. Congeniality" at the club last week—you or me?

ROBERT. Hannah, who are you telling to be quiet?

HANNAH. Quiet, Robert.

WILBUR. *(To Joanne.)* Afraid to answer? Huh? Who? Who was "Mr. Congeniality"? Tell me—were you "Mr. Congeniality"?

JENNY. *(To Wilbur.)* I don't think she stood a chance, Dad.

WILBUR. *(To Jenny.)* Who asked you, huh?

JENNY. "Mr. Congeniality," I think.

WILBUR. Don't be disrespectful.

AMA. We must begin Special Testimony! Who is first?

POPO. I talk.

JOANNE. Good.

POPO. Talk from here. *(She stands.)* Long time since we all come here like this. I remember long ago, family leave China—the boat storm, storm, storm, storm, all around, Hannah cry. I think, "Aaah, why we have to leave China, go to Philippines?" But I remember Jonah, when he did not obey God, only then seas become—ah—ah dangerous. And even after, after Jonah eaten by whale, God provide for him. So if God has plan for us, we live; if not *(She looks at Di-gou.)* we die. *(She sits.)* Okay. That's all. *(Everyone applauds.)*

AMA. Very good! Who is next?

ROBERT. I said, I'd be happy to—

HANNAH. How about Jenny?

JENNY. Me?

JOANNE. Sure, dear, c'mon.

JENNY. Oh...well...

POPO. *(To Di-gou.)* You see—she is so young, but her faith is old.

JENNY. After I do this, can I go see what's happened to Chester?

POPO. *(To Jenny.)* First, serve God.

ROBERT. Let her go.

POPO. Then, you may see about Chester.

JENNY. All right. *(She walks to the podium.)*

POPO. *(To Di-gou.)* I will tell you what each sentence meaning.

DI-GOU. I can understand quite well.

POPO. No. You are not Christian. You need someone—like announcer at baseball game—except announce for God.

JENNY. *(At podium, she begins testimony.)* First, I want to say that I love you all very much. I really do.

POPO. *(To Di-gou.)* That meaning is, she love God.

JENNY. And I appreciate what you've done for me.

POPO. *(To Di-gou.)* She love us because we show her God.

JENNY. But I guess there are certain times when even love isn't enough.

POPO. *(To Di-gou.)* She does not have enough love for you. You are not Christian.

JENNY. Sometimes, even love has its dark side.

POPO. *(To Di-gou.)* This is you.

JENNY. And when you find that side, sometimes you have to leave in order to come back in a better way.

POPO. *(To Di-gou.)* She cannot stand to be around you.

JENNY. Please. Remember what I said, and think about it later.

POPO. *(To Di-gou.)* You hear? Think!

JENNY. Thank you. *(Everyone applauds.)*

AMA. Good, good.

JENNY. Can I go now?

ROBERT. *(To Hannah.)* What was she talking about?

AMA. *(To Jenny.)* Soon, you can be best testifier—do testimony on TV.

JENNY. Can I go now?

JOANNE. All right, Jenny.

JENNY. Thanks. *(Exits.)*

ROBERT. *(To Popo.)* Why don't you interpret for *me?* I didn't understand what she was talking about. Not a bit.

POPO. Good.

ROBERT. Good? Don't you want me to be a better Christian?

POPO. No. Not too good. Do not want to live in same part of Heaven as you.

ROBERT. Why not? It'll be great, Popo. We can tell stories, sing—

POPO. In Heaven, hope you live in basement.

ROBERT. Basement? C'mon, Popo, I'm a celebrity. They wouldn't give me the basement. They'll probably recognize my diplomacy ability, make me ambassador.

JOANNE. To Hell?

ROBERT. Well, if that's the place they send ambassadors.

POPO. Good. You be ambassador.

AMA. Special Testimony! Who is next?

ROBERT. *(Asking to be recognized.)* Ama?

AMA. *(Ignoring him.)* Who is next?

ROBERT. Not me. I think Wilbur should speak.

AMA. *(Disgusted.)* Wilbur?

WILBUR. Me?

ROBERT. Yeah.

WILBUR. Well, I don't really...

ROBERT. Tell them, Wilbur. Tell them what kind of big stuffs happen to you. Tell them how important you are.

WILBUR. Well, I...

AMA. Would you...like to speak...Wilbur?

WILBUR. Well, I'd be honored, but if anyone else would rather...

ROBERT. We want to hear what you have to be proud of.

WILBUR. All right. *(Wilbur takes the podium; Ama scurries away.)* Uh—well, it's certainly nice to see this family reunion. Uh—last week, I was voted Mr. Congeniality at the club.

ROBERT. What papers was it in?

WILBUR. Huh?

ROBERT. Was it in the L.A. *Times?* Front page? Otis Chandler's paper?

HANNAH. *(A rebuff.)* Robert!

POPO. *(To Robert.)* Devotions is not question-and-answer for anyone except God.

ROBERT. God sometimes speaks through people, doesn't He?

POPO. He has good taste. Would not speak through you.

ROBERT. *(Undaunted, to Wilbur.)* Show me one newspaper clipping. Just one!

WILBUR. Well, besides the *Valley Green Sheet...*

ROBERT. The *Valley Green Sheet?* Who pays for that? Junk. People line their birdcages with it.

WILBUR. Well, I suppose from media standpoint, it's not that big a deal.

AMA. *(To Joanne.)* What means "congeniality"?

JOANNE. It means "friendly," sort of.

ROBERT. *(To Wilbur.)* So why are you talking about it? Waste our time?

WILBUR. Look, Robert, it's obviously a token of their esteem.

ROBERT. Junk stuffs. Little thing. Who cares?

AMA. *(To herself.)* "Mr. Friendly"?

ROBERT. It's embarrassing. What if clients say to me, "You're a bank president but your relative can only get into the *Valley Green Sheet?*"Makes me lose face. They think my relatives are bums.

AMA. *(To Joanne.)* He is "Mr. Friendly"?

WILBUR. Look, Robert, the business is doing real well. It's not like that's my greatest accomplishment.

AMA. *(To Joanne.)* How can he be "Mr. Friendly"? He always kill and laugh.

JOANNE. Mom!

ROBERT. *(To Wilbur.)* Does your business get in the paper?

WILBUR. Computer software happens to be one of the nation's fastest-growing—

ROBERT. So what? Lucky guess. Big deal.

WILBUR. It was an educated choice, not luck! *(Robert gets up, starts to head for the podium.)*

ROBERT. Anyone can make money in America. What's hard is to become...a celebrity.

WILBUR. You're not a celebrity!

ROBERT. Yes, I am. That's the new thing. See, I just wanted to say that— *(He nudges Wilbur off the podium, takes his place.)* —when I was kidnapped, I didn't know if I would live or die.

POPO. *(Turns and sees Robert at the podium.)* Huh?

JOANNE. Robert, forget it!

POPO. How did he get up there?

WILBUR. *(To Joanne.)* I'm perfectly capable of handling this myself.

POPO. He sneak up there while we are bored!

WILBUR. *(To Popo.)* I'm sorry you found my testimony boring.

ROBERT. *(To Wilbur.)* It was. *(To the assemblage.)* Now hear mine.

JOANNE. We've all heard it before.

HANNAH. *(To Robert.)* They're tired, dear. Get down.

ROBERT. Why? They listened to Wilbur's stuff. Boring. Junk.

JOANNE. "I didn't know if I would live or die." "I didn't know if I would live or die."

ROBERT. Di-gou, he hasn't heard. Have you, Di-gou?

DI-GOU. Is this when you didn't know if you would live or die?

ROBERT. How did—? Who told him?

POPO. I cannot think of enough ways to shoot him! Rifle! Arrows!

HANNAH. *(To Robert.)* Sit down!

ROBERT. But there's something new!

HANNAH. I think we better let him speak, or he'll never shut up.

ROBERT. She's right. I won't.

JOANNE. All right. Make it quick, Robert.

ROBERT. All right. As I was saying. I didn't know if I would live or die.

JOANNE. You lived.

ROBERT. But the resulting publicity has made me a celebrity. Every place I go, people come up to me—"Aren't you the one that got kidnapped?" When I tell them how much the ransom was, they can hardly believe it. They ask for my autograph. Now—here's the new thing. I met these clients last week, told them my story. Now, these guys are big shots and they say it would make a great movie. Yeah. No kidding. They made movies before. Not just regular movie, that's junk stuffs. We want to go where the big money is— we want to make mini-series for TV. Like "Shogun." I told them, they should take the story, spice it up a little, you know? Add some sex scenes—we were thinking that I could have some hanky-panky with one of my kidnappers—woman, of course—just for audience sake—like Patty Hearst. I told them I should be played by Marlon Brando. And I have the greatest title: "Not a Chinaman's Chance." Isn't that a great title? "Not a Chinaman's Chance." Beautiful. I can see the beginning already: I'm walking out of my office. I stop to help a man fixing a flat tire.

HANNAH. All right, dear. That's enough.

ROBERT. Meanwhile, my secretary is having sex with my kidnapper.

HANNAH. Kidnap! Kidnap! That's all I ever hear about!

ROBERT. But, Hannah, I didn't know if I would live or die.

HANNAH. I wish you'd never even been kidnapped.

JOANNE. Well, what about Wilbur?

WILBUR. Leave me out of this.

JOANNE. Wilbur, you could be kidnapped.

WILBUR. I know, I know. It just hasn't happened yet, that's all.

HANNAH. Listen, Joanne. Count your blessings. It's not that great a thing. If they live, they never stop talking about it.

ROBERT. But the publicity!—I sign newspapers all the time!

JOANNE. I'm just saying that Robert's not the only one worth kidnapping.

HANNAH. Joanne, no one's saying that.

AMA. Yes. We all desire Wilbur to be kidnapped also.

POPO. And Robert. Again. This time, longer.

JOANNE. I mean, Wilbur has a lot of assets.

ROBERT. Wilbur, maybe next time you can get kidnapped.

WILBUR. Never mind, honey.

JOANNE. You do.

WILBUR. I can defend myself.

ROBERT. But it takes more than assets to be kidnapped. You have to be cosmopolitan.

HANNAH. Hey, wait. What kind of example are we setting for Di-gou?

ROBERT. See? That's why I'm talking about it. To show Di-gou the greatness of America. I'm just an immigrant, Di-gou, an FOB—but in America, I get kidnapped.

HANNAH. I mean, a Christian example.

DI-GOU. Oh, do not worry about me. This is all very fascinating.

JOANNE. *(To Robert.)* So, you think you're cosmopolitan, huh?

ROBERT. I am. Before they let me loose, those kidnappers—they respected me.

JOANNE. They probably let you go because they couldn't stand to have you in their car.

POPO. Probably you sing to them.

ROBERT. No. They said, "We've been kidnapping a long time, but—"

JOANNE. Because we can't stand to have you in our house! *(Pause.)*

ROBERT. *(To Joanne.)* Now what kind of example are you setting for Di-gou?

WILBUR. Joanne, just shut up, okay?

HANNAH. *(To Di-gou.)* It's not always like this.

JOANNE. *(To Wilbur.)* You never let me talk! You even let him *(Refers to Robert.)* talk, but you never let me talk!

AMA. *(To Joanne.)* He *(Refers to Wilbur.)* cannot deprive you of right to speak. Look. No gun.

ROBERT. Joanne, I have to tell this because Di-gou is here.

DI-GOU. Me?

JOANNE. *(To Robert.)* You tell it to waiters!

ROBERT. Joanne, I want him *(Refers to Di-gou.)* to understand America. The American Dream. From rags to kidnap victim.

JOANNE. *(To Robert.)* Well, I don't like you making Di-gou think that Wilbur's a bum.

WILBUR. *(To Joanne.)* Dear, he doesn't think that.

JOANNE. *(To Di-gou.)* You see, don't you, Di-gou? This house. Wilbur bought this.

DI-GOU. It is a palace.

JOANNE. It's larger than Robert's.

HANNAH. Joanne, how can you sink to my husband's level?

ROBERT. My house would be larger, but we had to pay the ransom.

POPO. Waste of money.

JOANNE. Look, all of you always put down Wilbur. Well, look at what he's done.

WILBUR. *(To Joanne.)* Just shut up, all right?

JOANNE. *(To Wilbur.)* Well, if you're not going to say it.

WILBUR. I don't need you to be my PR firm.

ROBERT. *(To anybody.)* He doesn't have a PR firm. We do. Tops firm.

JOANNE. *(To Wilbur.)* Let me say my mind!

WILBUR. There's nothing in your mind worth saying.

JOANNE. What?

WILBUR. Face it, honey, you're boring.

AMA. *(To Wilbur.)* At least she does not torture!

WILBUR. Please! No more talking about torture, all right?

AMA. All right. I will be quiet. No need to torture me.

POPO. *(To Di-gou.)* This small family disagreement.

JOANNE. So I'm boring, huh?

WILBUR. *(To Joanne.)* Look, let's not do this here.

POPO. *(To Di-gou.)* But power of God will overcome this.

JOANNE. I'm boring—that's what you're saying?

HANNAH. Joanne! Not in front of Di-gou!

JOANNE. *(To Di-gou.)* All right. You're objective. Who do you think is more boring?

DI-GOU. Well, I can hardly—

WILBUR. Please, Joanne.

POPO. *(To Di-gou.)* Do you understand how power of God will overcome this?

JOANNE. He *(Refers to Wilbur.)* spends all his time with machines, and he calls me boring!

AMA. Di-gou, see the trials of this world?

WILBUR. *(To Joanne.)* Honey, I'm sorry, all right?

JOANNE. Sure, you're sorry.

AMA. *(To Di-gou.)* Argument, fight, no-good husbands.

WILBUR. "No-good husbands"? *(Robert, in disgust, exits into the house.)*

AMA. *(To Di-gou.)* Turn your eyes from this. *(Popo and Ama turn Di-gou's eyes from the fight.)*

JOANNE. *(To Wilbur.)* She's *(Refers to Ama.)* right, you know.

WILBUR. All right, honey, let's discuss this later.

JOANNE. Later! Oh, right. *(Wilbur runs off into the house; Joanne yells after him.)* When we're with *your* family, that's when you want to talk about my denting the Ferrari.

HANNAH. Joanne! Don't be so boring!

JOANNE. *(To Hannah.)* With *our* family, it's "later."

AMA. *(To Di-gou.)* Look up to God! *(Popo and Ama force Di-gou to look up.)*

DI-GOU. Please! *(Di-gou breaks away from the sisters' grip, but they knock him down.)*

POPO. Now—is time to join family in Heaven.

AMA. Time for you to return to God.

HANNAH. *(To Joanne.)* Look—they're converting Di-gou.

POPO. Return. Join us for eternity.

AMA. Pray now. *(Popo and Ama try to guide Di-gou to the neon cross.)*

DI-GOU. Where are we going?

AMA. He will wash you in blood of the lamb.

POPO. Like when you are a child. Now! You bow down!

HANNAH. Ask God for His forgiveness.

JOANNE. You won't regret it, Di-gou.

DI-GOU. Do you mind? *(He breaks away.)*

POPO. Why will you not accept Him?

AMA. There is no good reason.

DI-GOU. I want to take responsibility for my own life.

POPO. You cannot!

AMA. Satan is rule your life now.

DI-GOU. I am serving the people.

AMA. You are not.

POPO. You serve them, they all die, go to Hell. So what?

DI-GOU. How can you abandon China for this Western religion?

AMA. It is not.

POPO. God is God of all people.

DI-GOU. There is no God! *(Pause.)*

AMA. There is too much Communist demon in him. We must cast out demon.

POPO. Now, tie him on table.

DI-GOU. This is ridiculous. Stop this. *(The women grab Di-gou, tie him on the table.)*

POPO. We have too much love to allow demon to live.

DI-GOU. What?

POPO. *(To Joanne and Hannah who are hesitating.)* Now!

DI-GOU. You can't—!

POPO. Now! Or demon will escape!

AMA. We must kill demon.

POPO. Shoot him!

AMA. Kill for good.

POPO. Make demon into *jok!*

DI-GOU. This is barbaric! You live with the barbarians, you become one yourself!

POPO. Di-gou, if we do not punish your body, demon will never leave.

AMA. Then you will return to China.

POPO. And you will die.

AMA. Go to Hell.

POPO. And it will be too late.

DI-GOU. I never expected Chinese children to tie down their elders. *(Di-gou is now securely tied to the table.)*

HANNAH. All right. We're ready.

POPO. Now—you give your testimony.

DI-GOU. I'll just lie here and listen, thank you.

AMA. You tell of God's mercies to you.

JOANNE. How He let you out of China.

AMA. Where you are torture.

JOANNE. Whipped.

POPO. After thirty year, He let you out. Praise Him!

DI-GOU. I will never do such a thing!

HANNAH. If you wait too long, He'll lose patience.

POPO. Now—tell of your trip with See-goh-poh.

POPO. The trip which begin your faith.

DI-GOU. I was only eight years old. I don't remember.

POPO. Tell how many were convert on her tour.

HANNAH. Tell them, Di-gou.

DI-GOU. I cannot.

JOANNE. Why? Just tell the truth.

POPO. Tell how you saw the miracle of a great evangelist, great servant of God.

HANNAH. Tell them before they lose their patience.

DI-GOU. I'm sorry. I will not speak.

POPO. Then we are sorry, Di-gou, but we must punish your body. Punish to drive out the demon and make you speak.

HANNAH. Don't make them do this, Di-gou.

AMA. If you will not speak See-goh-poh's stories in language you know, we will punish you until you speak in tongue of fire. *(Ama hits Di-gou with an electrical cord, using it like a whip.)*

JOANNE. Please, Di-gou!

HANNAH. Tell them!

AMA. Our Lord was beat, nails drive through His body, for our sin. Your body must suffer until you speak the truth. *(Ama hits him.)*

HANNAH. Tell them, See-goh-poh was a great evangelist.

AMA. You were on her evangelism tour—we were not—you must remember her converts, her miracle. *(Hit.)*

JOANNE. Just tell them and they'll let you go!

AMA. Think of See-goh-poh! She is sit. *(Hit.)* Sit beside God. He is praising her! Praise her for her work in China. *(Chester enters the tennis court; he looks into the sunroom and sees Ama hit Di-gou.)* She is watching you! *(Hit. Chester tries to get into the sunroom, but the glass door is locked. He bangs on it, but everyone inside stands shocked at Ama's ritual, and no one notices him. He exits off the tennis court, running.)* Praying for you! Want you to tell her story! *(Hit.)* We will keep you in float. Float for one second between life and death. Float until you lost will to hold to either—hold to anything at all. (Ama quickly slips the cord around Di-gou's neck, begins pulling on it. Joanne and Hannah run to get Ama off of Di-gou. Chester enters from the house, with Jenny close behind him. He pulls Ama off of Di-gou.)*

CHESTER. Ama! Stop it! *(Di-gou suddenly breaks out of his bonds and rises up on the table. He grabs Chester. The barbecue bursts into flames. Di-gou, holding onto Chester, begins speaking in tongues.)*

AMA. *(Looking up from the ground.)* He is speaking in tongues! He has returned! *(Everyone falls to their knees. As Di-gou's tongues continue, Chester is suddenly filled with words, and begins interpreting Di-gou's babbling.)*

CHESTER. Di-gou at eight goes with See-goh-poh on her first evangelism tour. Di-gou and See-goh-poh traveling through the summer heat to a small village in Fukien. Sleeping in the straw next to See-goh-poh. Hearing a sound. A human sound. A cry in my sleep. Looking up and seeing a fire. A fire and See-goh-poh. See-goh-poh is naked. Naked and screaming. Screaming with legs spread so far apart. So far that a mouth opens up. A mouth between her legs. A mouth that is throwing up blood. See-goh-poh's hands making a baby out of the blood. See-goh-poh hits the blood baby. Hits the baby and the baby cries. Watching the baby at See-goh-poh's breast. Hearing the sucking. *(Ama and Popo spring up.)*

POPO. Such a thing never happened!

AMA. See-goh-poh never did this!

POPO. This is not tongues. This is not God. This is demon!

CHESTER. Sucking. Praying. Sucking. Squeezing. Crying.

AMA. He is possess by demon!

CHESTER. Biting. Blood. Milk.

POPO. Both have the demon!

CHESTER. Blood and milk. Blood and milk running down.

AMA. *(To the other women.)* You pray.

CHESTER. Running down, further and further down.

POPO. We must cast out the demon! *(Di-gou's tongues slowly become English, first overlapping, then overtaking Chester's translation. Chester becomes silent and exhausted, drops to the ground.)*

CHESTER and DI-GOU. Down. Down and into the fire. The fire down there. The fire down there. *(Di-gou breaks the last of his bonds, gets off the table.)*

DI-GOU. *(To the sisters.)* Your stories are dead now that you know the truth.

AMA. We have faith. We know our true family stories.

DI-GOU. You do not know your past.

AMA. Are you willing to match your stories against ours? *(Di-gou indicates his willingness to face Ama, and the two begin a ritualistic battle. Popo supports Ama by speaking in tongues. Ama and Di-gou square off in seated positions, facing one another.)* We will begin. How many rooms in our house in Amoy?

94

DI-GOU. Eighteen. How many bedrooms?

AMA. Ten. What year was it built?

DI-GOU. 1893. What year was the nineteenth room added?

AMA. 1923.

DI-GOU. On whose instructions.

AMA. See-goh-poh.

DI-GOU. What year did See-goh-poh die?

AMA. 1945. What disease?

DI-GOU. Malaria. How many teeth was she missing?

AMA. Three.

DI-GOU. What villages were on See-goh-poh's evangelism tour? *(Silence.)* Do you know?

AMA. She preached to all villages in Fukien.

DI-GOU. Name one. *(Silence.)* Do you know? Your stories don't know. It never happened.

AMA. It did! What year was she baptized? *(Silence.)* What year was she baptized?

DI-GOU. She was never baptized.

AMA. You see? You don't remember.

DI-GOU. Never baptized.

AMA. You see? You don't remember.

DI-GOU. Never baptized.

AMA. It was 1921. Your stories do not remember.

DI-GOU. Who was converted on her evangelism tour?

AMA. Perhaps five hundred or more.

DI-GOU. Who? Name one. *(Silence.)*

AMA. It is not important.

DI-GOU. You see? It never happened.

AMA. It did.

DI-GOU. You do not remember. You do not know the past. See-goh-poh never preached.

AMA. How can you say this?

DI-GOU. She traveled.

AMA. To preach.

DI-GOU. To travel.

AMA. She visited many—

DI-GOU. I was there! She was thrown out—thrown out on her evangelism tour when she tried to preach. *(Silence.)*

AMA. It does not matter.

DI-GOU. You forced her to invent the stories.

AMA. We demand nothing!

DI-GOU. You expected! Expected her to convert all Amoy!

AMA. She did!

DI-GOU. Expected many miracles.

AMA. She did! She was a great—

DI-GOU. Expected her not to have a baby.

AMA. She had no husband. She had no baby. This is demon talk. Demon talk and lie.

DI-GOU. She turned away from God.

AMA. We will never believe this!

DI-GOU. On her tours she could please you and see China. *(Popo's tongues become weaker; she starts to falter.)*

AMA. See-goh-poh was a great—

DI-GOU. Only on her tours could she see both China and her baby.

AMA. She was a great...a great evangelist...many...

DI-GOU. Where is she buried?

AMA. ...many miracle...

DI-GOU. She is not buried within the walls of the church in Amoy.

AMA. ...many miracle a great evangelist... *(Popo collapses.)*

DI-GOU. In her last moment, See-goh-poh wanted to be buried in Chinese soil, not Christian soil. You don't know. You were in the Philippines. *(Pause.)* I come to bring you back to China. Come, sisters. To the soil you've forsaken with ways born of memories, of stories that never happened. Come, sisters. The stories written on your face are the ones you must believe. *(Ama rises from her chair.)*

AMA. We will never believe this! *(She collapses back into her chair, closes her eyes. Silence.)*

DI-GOU. Sisters? *(Silence.)* Sisters! *(Jenny, Chester, Joanne, Hannah, and Di-gou stare at the two inert forms.)*

CHESTER. Jenny! Jenny! *(Jenny goes to Chester's side.)*

JOANNE. Hannah? Hannah—come here. *(Hannah does not move.)*

HANNAH. I see.

JOANNE. No! Come here!

HANNAH. I know, Joanne. I see.

DI-GOU. Once again. Once again my pleas are useless. But now—this is the last time. I have given all I own. *(Popo and Ama have died. Di-gou picks up his suitcase and the Chinese toys, heads for the door.)*

JOANNE. *(To Di-gou.)* Are you leaving?

DI-GOU. Now that my sisters have gone, I learn. No one leaves America. And I desire only to drive an American car—very fast—down an American freeway. *(Di-gou exits.)*

JOANNE. *(Yelling after him.)* This is our home, not yours! Why didn't you stay in China! This is not your family! *(Jenny starts to break away from Chester, but he hangs onto her. Joanne turns, sees the figures of Ama and Popo.)* Wilbur! Wilbur, come here!

JENNY. *(To Chester.)* Let go of me! Get away! *(She breaks away from Chester.)* I don't understand this, but whatever it is, it's ugly and it's awful and it causes people to die. It causes people to die and I don't want to have anything to do with it. *(Jenny runs out onto the tennis court and away. On her way, she passes Robert, who has entered onto the court. Robert walks into the sunroom. Silence.)*

ROBERT. What's wrong with her? She acts like someone just died. *(Silence. He pulls up a chair next to Chester.)* Let's chit-chat, okay?

CHESTER. Sure, Dad.

ROBERT. So, how's Dorrie? *(Silence.)* How much they paying you in Boston? *(Silence.)* Got any new newspaper clipping's? *(Silence. Chester gets up, picks up his suitcase, walks onto the tennis court, and shuts the glass doors. Ama and Popo lie in the center of the room. Joanne and Hannah stare at them. Robert sits, staring off into space. Chester turns around, looks through the glass door onto the scene. The lights begin to dim until there is a single spotlight on Chester's face, standing where Di-gou stood at the beginning of the play. The shape of Chester's face begins to change.)*

CURTAIN

PROPERTY LIST

ACT I
Old suitcase, with Chinese toys & small Chinese flag
Barbecue, with burned chickens etc.
Long fork
Wire-mesh box
Empty laundry basket
Green suitcase
Newspaper clipping (Robert)
Handbook (Di-Gou)
Tray of Chinese food
Tennis rackets
Tennis ball machine
Violin, in case
Neon cross

ACT II
Podium
Table
Electrical cord